A NEW
WORLD
TRADE
CENTER

A NEW WORLD TRADE CENTER

DESIGN PROPOSALS
FROM LEADING ARCHITECTS WORLDWIDE

Max Protetch

ReganBooks
An Imprint of HarperCollins*Publishers*

To my children, Nicola and David Protetch,

and their mother, Heather Nicol,

who have so bravely

dealt with the changes in their lives

since September 11

Editor's note: With the exception of the text for Samuel Mockbee's proposal, which was written by Max Protetch, the text for each proposal was written by the individual architects, artists, and firms.

A NEW WORLD TRADE CENTER. Copyright © 2002 by Max Protetch. All rights reserved. Printed in the United States of America. No part of this book may be used or reproduced in any manner whatsoever without written permission except in the case of brief quotations embodied in critical articles and reviews. For information address HarperCollins Publishers Inc., 10 East 53rd Street, New York, NY 10022.

HarperCollins books may be purchased for educational, business, or sales promotional use. For information please write: Special Markets Department, HarperCollins Publishers Inc., 10 East 53rd Street, New York, NY 10022.

FIRST EDITION

Designed by Kate Nichols

Printed on acid-free paper

Library of Congress Cataloging-in-Publication Data has been applied for.

ISBN 0-06-052016-7

02 03 04 05 06 QW 10 9 8 7 6 5 4 3 2 1

Contents

Introduction

Like others who experienced the events of September 11 firsthand, I was moved to make a positive contribution. I couldn't deny an irrepressible interest in what would replace the World Trade Center. I knew most architects and many others were thinking along similar lines, though they probably felt, as I did, that such thoughts were unseemly given the horrible circumstances of that day. However, I realized that in four months' time there would be a great deal of pressure on those who would have the power to control the future of the World Trade Center site, and that the drive to maximize commercial square footage might lead to knee-jerk architectural responses. I felt moved to utilize my experience in a way that would allow me to help prevent the sacrifice of great architectural opportunities in the name of "business as usual," and I believed that the site demanded a lasting monument to human creativity and resilience as a response to the attack.

As someone who has owned an art gallery all of his adult life, and who has, for the last twenty years, been a dealer in architectural drawing as well as contemporary art, I felt it was only natural to begin to identify the most creative and diverse group of international architects, to think about how these firms and individuals might envision the redevelopment of the World Trade Center site. At times I have also acted as a consultant to individuals and corporations, helping them to choose the architect who best matches their program and personality. In this case, I began to think about casting as wide a net as possible, to bring to the public the greatest array of architectural possibilities for downtown Manhattan. I knew that seeing these possibilities together in a gallery would be a cathartic experience not only for myself and for the artists and architects who created the proposals, but also for the larger public. In late September, however, I wasn't aware just how deeply we all needed this kind of positive and forward-thinking activity in the months following the terrorist attack.

Like most New Yorkers, I wished to do something positive and helpful. However, due to the city's incredible outpouring of support, donations of food and clothing were quickly discouraged, and even blood donors were being turned away. I began to realize that I was able to best make my contribution based upon the circumstances of my occupation and the gallery's focus on architecture. This put me in the unique position to quickly mount an exhibition that examined the ideas that September 11 was generating in the architectural world. For a museum to create a show like this one, it would need confirmation of every object from every participant well before announcing the show to the public. My gallery, on the other hand, was able to announce the show long before we were even finished inviting participants and determining the amount of work we would receive. Because the gallery operates outside the realm of any other institution, and because I am an art dealer who has extensive experience dealing with architecture's "major players," we were able to react quickly to the situation and begin work on the show in late September.

The first step was to determine exactly whom we wanted to invite. Ordinarily, when a gallery organizes an invitational show, it invites a few artists whose work engages the show's theme in a particularly interesting way. In this case it was important to invite not only the established, building architects, but also those who are most clearly defining the theoretical and technological issues of our time, as well as those creative architects who will help define architecture in the near future. For a variety of reasons, it was also very important to me that the search for participants be an international one. Since the program was to develop a design for a site that symbolized world trade, and since the victims of the September 11 attacks hailed from many nations and walks of life, it seemed essential to assert that architectural creativity is not defined or limited by national borders.

We also had to consider the fact that only a percentage of those whom we invited would agree to participate in the show. The challenge we were proposing was a very difficult one. We were asking architects to create a design for a project with no identifiable client or program, and essentially no limits. On top of this, we were operating at a time of major emotional flux. Many of the architects were busy dealing with the repercussions of a changed business climate, including canceled projects and increased costs and time associated with transportation and security. In addition, creative architecture is never the result of one person's work at a drawing board or computer, but typically requires the resources of an entire office to attend to design details. We were asking architects to commit resources to a project without compensation, and to stick their necks out and open themselves to criticism for even participating in the show.

With this in mind, we invited 125 architects in hopes of finding about fifty participants. We ended up with sixty individuals and firms, but not without some major arm-twisting. Many of the invitees, especially some from Europe, felt uncomfortable proposing designs to a recently traumatized America. And in many cases those who were uncomfortable but willing to participate were only interested in suggesting concepts for memorials. On the other hand, I saw the exhibition as part of an optimistic American vision, and hoped the designs would address a variety of uses. What better memorial to those who perished than great architecture, architecture that can accommodate business, residential, and green spaces, and that can revitalize downtown Manhattan?

I also began to realize that people across the world were affected by September 11 almost as deeply as New Yorkers. Watching on television as airliners controlled by terrorists flew into the World Trade Center and the Pentagon, the American and international public at large became suddenly aware of the symbolic, political, economic, and social importance of architecture. In the terrorists' eyes, these buildings were targets that symbolized American economic and cultural dominance. If the general public was now aware of the way in which architecture truly represents a culture and a civilization, I realized that there might indeed be a wide audience for a more inventive and creative architecture in lower Manhattan. More than anything else, it has been this idea that has kept me excited about our project: to think that we might be able to impact policy changes downtown and prevent "business as usual" when it comes to architecture and planning.

I would define great architecture much in the way I would define great art. The most important artists are those who teach us to see in new ways, and the most memorable architects are those who teach us to reevaluate our relationships to the spaces we inhabit. In many ways, architecture is a more complicated case in this regard, since it must anticipate future uses while remaining firmly rooted in the programs and contingencies of the present. In addition, it must deal in very real terms with issues of safety, ecology, and relation to the surrounding context.

As I continued to think about these ideas, as well as the remarkable architects we were inviting to participate in the show and the designs they might propose, I realized that New York, the financial and cultural capital of the world, was a city of good buildings, but not great ones. I began to think of the excuses for this situation: "It can't be built, people won't want to inhabit avant-garde architecture, the building codes are too strict and too narrow, the costs of advanced architecture can't be supported. . . ." None of them held water. We live in a world that has become sophisticated in its appreciation of good architecture and the way in which it can transform our urban environments. I believe that corporations and individuals are aware of the value of associations with the greatest architects of the time, and that they would pay an even greater premium to work and live at or near the World Trade Center if great architects were responsible for its redesign. As a result, the new downtown New York would become even more desirable as a center for commerce, finance, housing, and recreation. The apartment buildings recently completed by Richard Meier in the Greenwich Village section of New York are a good example of what can happen when a world-renowned architect takes on a residential project. Though the buildings are not revolutionary, they are well-designed structures whose units sold at a premium that more than paid for the added expenses of more advanced building techniques.

It is perhaps easier to approach an idea like this when you put it into historical context. Just think if there were a situation somewhat analogous to this one fifty years ago, with a sudden opportunity to redesign a large-scale urban space, and an enlightened group of individuals deciding who would build, people powerful enough to invite the best architects of their time to work together on a single site. Imagine if Saarinen, Aalto, Le Corbusier, Kahn, Mies, and Wright were some of those who were invited to participate. How might that have changed New York, influenced its population, and created a new understanding of and appreciation for architecture as a primary force that shapes culture and human relations?

Unlike Rockefeller Center, which was designed by one very good architect, and the United Nations headquarters, which was designed by a collaborative team, the World Trade Center site provides possibilities for several of the best minds to design individual buildings that would re-create the fabric of lower Manhattan and give form to the most advanced architectural thought of our time.

Architecture is a most complicated art; it is imaginative and abstract, but it deals directly with all the social, political, and economic issues of its time. Furthermore, it is constantly reacting and relating to a changing and expanding technological base. Great architects are the most exciting jugglers, always keeping a diversity of issues in the air simultaneously, maintaining their creative vision while meeting requirements imposed by budgets, scheduling, codes, and client programs. It is important that we keep this in mind as the first phases of lower Manhattan's redesign are immediately upon us. Architectural professionals, academics, and forward-thinking engineers should play active roles as the Metropolitan Transit Authority and the Port Authority plan for a new central railroad station and the private Westfield Corporation, which owns the commercial leases for the underground space at the World Trade Center, pursues the rebuilding of the subterranean shopping plazas. Even if these sites remain below grade, it is essential that we advocate for advanced design, so that an imaginative spirit can be the guiding force for the network of spaces that will be the entryway to the World Trade Center for all visitors arriving via subways and commuter trains. With intelligently planned links to area airports, which should be a primary consideration, the World Trade Center could truly reassert its position as an international gateway to New York.

We are now faced with the opportunity to present a grand vision for a renewed urban center. Above grade, there have been proposals to slow the rate of development by dividing it into different sectors and reinstating the city grid. A competition could be held to decide upon the designs for each of the sites. Since this process would take place over a number of years, there would be ample time to consider and select the best proposals, as well as multiple opportunities to reassess a changing economic situation. In this way, we would avoid creating an excess of office space that the economy could not support, while maintaining the flexibility to create more space, as it becomes needed in the near future.

A consensus has been building in favor of reinstating the street grid, not only because it allows for a more sensitive building and planning process, but also because it seems to provide the best chance for achieving a truly mixed-use urban situation. A combination of residential and commercial structures in close proximity, featuring ground-level retail, open space, and accessible mass transportation, has brought life to other areas of the city.

Of course there is one major addition to these elements that should become a part of any eventual World Trade Center design: a prominent memorial. All of us understand the need for a memorial, so strongly stated by the families of those who lost their lives on September 11, and so strongly felt by citizens of the city, the country, and the world. However, I remain convinced that the most fitting memorial is a living city that would reflect our best aspirations, and that would inspire future generations. It is my hope that such a city would also result in a pronounced formal presence for the New York skyline. The Twin Towers lent a strong, symbolic coherence to lower Manhattan, and we all feel the lack of such a presence since their destruction, even though they weren't particularly great buildings.

There is a need in New York for bold, recognizable forms that reflect contemporary design and technology. Frank Lloyd Wright, when accused of designing futuristic architecture, said with typical immodesty that he was merely utilizing the technology of his time as opposed to that of the past, as others were currently doing. Wright recognized that great contemporary architecture is often perceived as futuristic or unfamiliar at the moment of its creation. He also recognized that the most successful buildings are those that anticipate the demands of the future by reflecting the most advanced thought, methods, and materials. It is crucial that such forward-looking architecture is created in lower Manhattan, so that New York can continue to grow as the world's financial and cultural capital. Only by recognizing this incredible opportunity for renewal can the destruction of September 11 be properly memorialized.

—MAX PROTETCH WITH STUART KRIMKO

Balthazar Korab began working as Minoru Yamasaki's photographer in 1958, and was in close design consultation with him. He documented the World Trade Center project's development from its inception in 1962 through the completion of the building. Korab studied architecture in Hungary and France, and worked with Frank Lloyd Wright, Eero Saarinen, and Le Corbusier as an architect in the 1950s. He was awarded the AIA Medal for Architectural Photography in 1964.

Balthazar Korab

Celebration of a Forward-Looking Spirit

In 1962, after considering several other architects to design the World Trade Center, the New York Port Authority chose Minoru Yamasaki and a great celebration took place in Troy, Michigan. I was there, and followed the development for the next fifteen years. I was witness and part of the tireless effort of the study, beyond my role as Yamasaki's photographer. The hundred or so schemes were slowly narrowed down to the two-tower, five-acre plaza that would be built. The heroic dimensions were adopted after long soul searching, projecting a symbolic monument for a new millennium that was to lead to world peace through global trade. This leap of faith met with a mixed reception from the critics. But with the passing years the Twin Towers became an essential feature of New York's skyline, reminding us of the gradual acceptance of the Eiffel Tower by the Parisians. The World Trade Center generated new energies, new life for Manhattan's downtown. Those energies grew to universal strength as a response to the September 11 tragedy. Undefeated, New Yorkers and the whole world rallied, showing solidarity in fighting the criminal calamity of terrorism.

I am proud to be a part of Max Protetch's initiative to celebrate a forward-looking spirit by inviting architects to present their visions for Ground Zero.

1100 Architect is the New York–based firm of David Piscuskas and Juergen Riehm. Since the practice was founded in 1983, their work has demonstrated a contemporary sensibility that is at once elegant, sophisticated, and inviting. The skillful use and manipulation of light and unexpected use of materials for which 1100 is recognized are continually at play in the varied projects undertaken by the firm. Within this fluent language, the architects forgo pre-set conclusions in order to serve each project, "whether free-standing construction, renovation, or the development of raw environment," through its own process of discovery. Key projects include the AIA-awarded Little Red School House/Elizabeth Irwin High School, the Robert Mapplethorpe Foundation, the MoMA Design Store, and the Irish Hunger Memorial in Battery Park City, slated for completion in July 2002.

1100 Architect

Between Permanence and Fragility

Our proposal acknowledges the tragedy that occurred on this site, the enduring presence of the victims who perished on September 11, and the phantom presence of the World Trade towers. Our thoughts were dictated by the phantoms of the towers; the scheme does not attempt to replace the towers literally. Their footprints are deep vessels filled with water to their original seven-story depth and become pools for reflection. The space—an absence—between the two pools is still redolent with the vibration of what used to be two mammoth buildings. We worked with this ten-foot-wide separation between the east face of the North Tower and the west face of the South Tower to conceive of a simple, vertical structure that rises to the height of the original buildings without attempting to mimic them. Two architectural planes radiate from that structure, each plane touching one of the reflecting pools. They comprise a series of passages that ascend as multiple paths open to, but protected from, the sky, the city, and the elements. A skeletal architecture is created—a wall of paths—that oscillates between permanence and temporality, clad in large panels of glass. The number of panels of glass totals the number of victims. Glass, a provocative material made through fire, is both fragile and resilient, but is neither liquid nor solid, neither alive nor dead. Human life is fragile, the impression of human life enduring. The panels of glass accord the opportunity for each of the victims to be remembered—distinctly, individually—and for the visitor to think, to see, to look through the remembrances of each of the victims to the living world beyond this place and this event.

On the ground, what we have conceived allows for the creation of a humane plaza. A portion of West Street would be recessed below surface grade, allowing people to traverse the site to the river, to move from water to water. The plaza also makes a site receptive to commercial development, hence the presence of two fifty- to sixty-story buildings to the north and east sides of the site. They help define an open urban place, an intersection between people and architecture, between the permanence and the fragility of life.

Raimund Abraham was born in Lienz, Austria, in 1933. He emigrated to the United States in 1964. In 1971 he moved to New York, where he has taught at Cooper Union ever since. Abraham has received various awards for his architectural designs, among them first prizes for the Rainbow Plaza in Niagara Falls, New York, for the International Building Exhibition in West Berlin, and for the Times Square Tower. In 1992, Abraham made international news when he won the competition to design the new Austrian Cultural Forum in midtown Manhattan.

Raimund Abraham

Zero Zones

Three inhabitable concrete slabs of 880 feet long, 110 feet wide, and 550 feet tall run north–south, between Vesey and Liberty Streets, 110 feet apart.

At the time of each plane hitting the towers and the collapse of each tower on September 11, 2001—at 8:46 A.M., 9:02 A.M., 9:59 A.M., and 10:28 A.M.—the exact position of the sun is located and fixed at the lateral angle from true east of 28.5 degrees, 32.7 degrees, 47.2 degrees, and 56.5 degrees.

Thirty-three-foot-wide and 550-foot-high passages are cut east–west through the three slabs at the centerlines of the lateral angles of the sun, marking and signifying the memory of the events from September 11 forever.

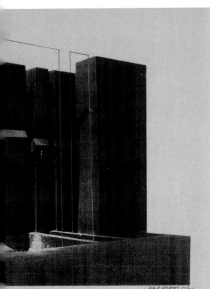

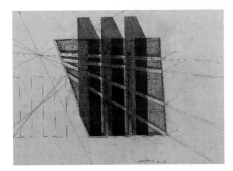

Vito Acconci's work began as fiction and poetry, which treated the page as a self-enclosed space for writer and reader to travel through. His first work in an art context, in the late sixties and early seventies, used performance, film, and video as instruments of self-analysis and person-to-person relationships. In the mid-eighties, the work became architecture, landscape architecture, and furniture design; at the end of the eighties, he started Acconci Studio, bringing together a group of architects who design projects for streets and plazas, gardens and parks, building lobbies, and transportation centers.

Acconci Studio

A Building Full of Holes

A building riddled with holes—a building preshot, pre-blown-out, preexploded . . . From the original site, the building is extruded to a height of 110 stories; the unnecessary office footage, the extra volume, is blown away . . .

A hole is a tube is a cone . . . The cones form the building's public spaces. Instead of being around or beside the building, they run through the middle of the building, intertwined with private spaces . . . You enter the public space through the open end of a cone at ground level, or from an office floor above . . .

The public spaces are exterior spaces inside the building; you see through the building—light streams through the building, like spotlights—it rains and snows through the building . . . The interior of each cone is lined with walkways, ramps, and stairways; these passages are parks (plantings, waterfalls, benches) and plazas and streets (food stands, markets, performance areas) . . .

A Building Made of Holes

The holes, cones, and tubes are the structure of the building . . . One tube intersects another; one may spiral around the interior of one tube and then meander into another, walking in the middle of offices but remaining outside of them . . . The building elevators cross through the tubes and bypass the public spaces . . .

WTC MEMORIAL
ADJMI
01

Morris Adjmi began working with Aldo Rossi in Milan, Italy, after obtaining his architectural degree from Tulane University in 1981. In 1986, Adjmi partnered with Aldo Rossi and opened Studio di Architettura in New York City, collaborating on designs for the Hotel Il Palazzo in Fukuoka, Japan, which received an AIA Honor Award, and the Celebration Office Complex in Orlando, Florida. In 1993, Adjmi founded the architecture and design firm MAP with partner Lisa Mahar. As the director of architecture at MAP, he has completed a wide range of interior projects for Amster Yard, Fallon, and Publicis.

Morris Adjmi

A Skyscraper Wrapped in the Flag

My proposal for the World Trade Center site uses the American flag as a building block for a large tower structure. Historically the flag has been used in troubled times to rally the nation and unite its diverse citizens. In the days and weeks following the disaster, the American flag emerged as a universal image of unity. I felt that this was an appropriate symbol to memorialize the loss of life and create hope for the future.

I thought of this building in terms of the overall image but also in terms of its use. Rather than fill the building with floor after floor of office space, I envisioned the building as an enormous cultural center. Out of the chaos of the attack, the building would provide a place to memorialize the tragedy and inspire people.

The superstructure of the building is wrapped with enormous images of the American flag. This skin would be connected to the structure in a manner that would make floor divisions indiscernible. In this way, the image will transcend the scale of a normal building, even though it is organized like a prototypical skyscraper with its wedding cake design.

Established in January 1997, Marwan Al-Sayed Architects Ltd. is a young and growing architectural design studio committed to a new standard of design excellence and construction. Based on principal architect Marwan Al-Sayed's extensive background of travel, the studio has successfully merged a conceptual, poetically driven design aesthetic with an extensive background and deep interest in building and construction. The House of Earth and Light in Phoenix, Arizona, completed in 2000, was selected to be in the National Design Triennial at the Cooper-Hewitt National Design Museum in New York City in March of 2000, a national survey of groundbreaking work in the fields of architecture, industrial and product design, graphics, film, and fashion.

Marwan Al-Sayed

Beauty and Creation Overcome Death

I began to ask myself what would be an appropriate response to all the death and destruction and pain caused by the events of that day. Beauty is the word that kept staring me in the face. Beauty—a form of sublime beauty—is the only possible response that I felt could begin the process of healing and also signal to the world the ability of creation to overcome death, destruction, and the evil acts of men.

The State of Things

I thus began by imagining five slender towers emerging from the site's perimeter, where there were once two. Like tall plants or grasses reemerging from the solid bedrock of earth, I envision them being driven by their thirst for sun and light. I imagine the towers being able to change their inner and outer skins; adapting to the weather, to the seasons, to the time of day, to the mood of the occupants, or of the city, or the nation, to holidays, and to events around the world. With this in mind, the site can become a kind of monumental marker, a sort of urban collective receptor and transmitter of the state of things.

Color, Emotion, and Art

Imagine, for instance, the towers glowing, ethereal frost-white with a glowing yellow chamber from floors 54 to 85 on a hot, humid summer day. Then imagine the same towers a deep crimson red on a cold blustery January day. Individual towers would change color and depth of transparency based on the events within the

buildings. And with New York being the artistic capital of the world, I can envision the towers being given over periodically to artists of great caliber to control as a giant three-dimensional painting or sculpture.

"Nano-Towers"

I have long been fascinated with composite materials, especially carbon fiber. Though it is used currently as a high-strength composite in sports and aviation, its use as a building material has been hampered by its brittleness when compressed. Recent discoveries have taken carbon fiber structures and rolled them into forms at the molecular level that immensely increase their strength. With the advancement of fiber optics as well, there may be a day when an ultrathin structure (a kind of spiderweb of material) will not only serve as the support structure, but also deliver sunlight from the sky directly into the depths of the building. This technology will support a building in which the skin can be reconfigured molecularly at the touch of a switch, to change, for instance, from a somber black to a glorious magenta.

The Monument and the Memorial

By making the towers more slender and by placing them at the east and west perimeter, I have attempted to free up the majority of the site, and to open it up to the southern sun. This large void, six stories in the air, would become the space of the memorial. A giant cascade of steps made of grass on the north and south sides, practically Mayan in scale and mystery, would take one from the street level up into this central void space. Intended as a giant twelve-acre blanket of grass, the purity of this space and the ability to simply lie down on the soft, moist grass would be a healing act unto itself. For in the midst of the financial district, the offering of a grass plain would be a statement of calm and serenity, where individuals or groups could gather to remember or celebrate the lives lost at the site. From here one can enter a chamber in each of the five towers. This is the true memorial space itself. Measuring only twenty feet wide by eighty feet long, the space rises the full height of the towers to an opening to the sky. This colossal space, where I envision all sense of scale and time distorted, would bring visitors face-to-face with the scale of the tragedy and the immensity of the void to be filled.

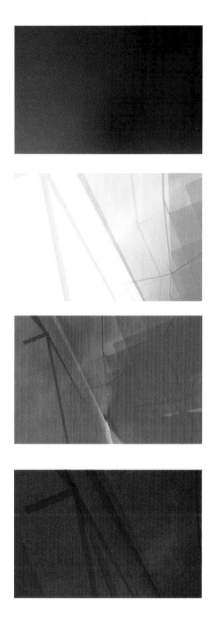

Allied Works Architecture's form of architectural inquiry often leads to exploration on the borders of various disciplines. The firm seeks out and explores conceptual precedents beyond the history of architecture, exploring the fields of land and installation art, enjoying the collaboration of artists, engineers, and landscape architects. Principal and founder Brad Cloepfil worked in New York, Los Angeles, and Switzerland for ten years before establishing Allied Works Architecture in Portland, Oregon, in 1994.

Allied Works Architecture

A Room in the Sky

We do not propose the design of a building, but an embodiment of aspirations for the site and the city.

Our initial motivations were: to create an urban space, not a spectacle, a sculptural object, or a symbolic memorial, but a resonant void in the city that will be filled with the activities of life; to repair the body of the city, rebuilding the urban fabric of downtown and transforming the place of individual work into a collective presence; and to provide rooms in which people would be able to come together for celebration, music, theater, and all forms of art, as well as for worship, contemplation, and reflection. A central feature would be a room for memory, an empty room in the sky to be filled with the thoughts and acts that sustain the spirit of those lost.

The project proposes occupying the site in specific ways. We have attempted to fill the site with people, while maintaining a sense of the void. We have repaired the fabric of lower Manhattan by reconnecting its streets and building new office space that extends the density and scale of its surroundings. Through this transparent labyrinth of new buildings we have created a large public square filled at various heights with collective spaces. We connect people back to the street, but also allow them to occupy the site in its entirety. This is accomplished through a series of "streets" on the third floor, on the tenth floor, and on the roof of the entire site. Our goal is to create a monumental presence; not an absence, but a space for the life of the city.

Perhaps we can use this tragedy as an opportunity to think of buildings as more than new shapes and objects. In the way we choose to build, we can create new spaces and new experiences to inspire a thoughtful and hopeful life.

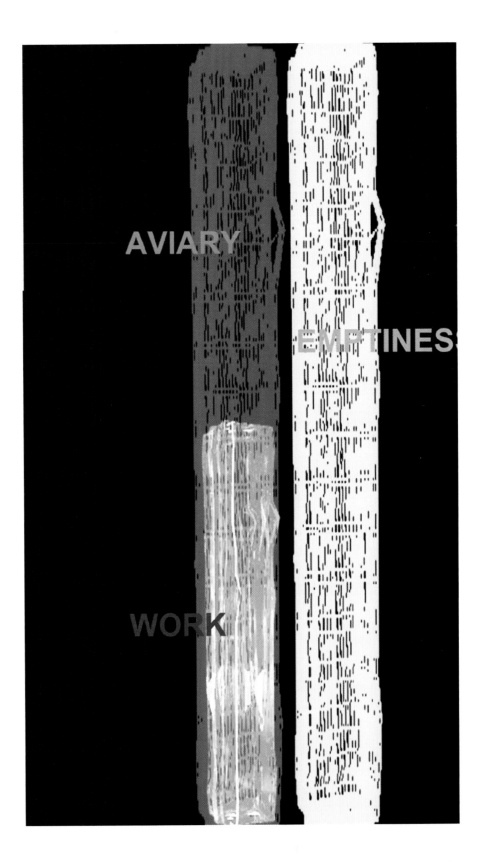

AVIARY

EMPTINESS

WORK

Will Alsop belongs to a generation of modern British architects who follow no single school of theory. Observing the practical conclusion of modernist tenets in elegant engineering exercises, he has fought for the assertion of individual creativity in architecture, in the belief that it can contribute to the lives of people and communities. Current projects for Alsop Architects include the master plan of central Rotterdam for the Rotterdam city council; the C/Plex Cultural and Arts Centre in West Bromwich, England; and a new building for the Ontario College of Art and Design, Toronto.

Will Alsop

An Office and an Aviary

My proposal suggests an exploration of the ambiance of the vision of the Trade Center site. I propose that the towers be replaced by similar structures, except that the new towers would be twice the height. One of these two towers would remain an office building, while the other would be an empty tower housing an aviary.

Winka Dubbeldam is the principal of Archi-Tectonics, NYC, founded in 1994. In 2001 she received an Emerging Voice award from the New York City Architectural League. Archi-Tectonics has completed several residential and commercial spaces in Manhattan. Archi-Tectonics was a participant in two exhibitions at the Museum of Modern Art, *The Unprivate House* (1999) and *Young Architects* (2001), and in the Archi-Lab conferences of 2000 and 2001 in Orléans, France.

Archi-Tectonics

Flex-City, NYC 1991–2001–2012: 81 Scenarios for Lower Manhattan Event

The invitation to participate in the exhibit at Max Protetch Gallery, *A New World Trade Center,* brought up mixed reactions. After a global terrorist act like the destruction of the World Trade Center, it is not easy to even begin to think of a replacement. At that point a rethinking seemed relevant, not a replacement or rebuilding of the Twin Towers; a rethinking not only of the changing urban conditions and the future development of this area, but of new architectural typologies. After all, the towers were not destroyed because they were high and great architecture, they were attacked as symbols of world power. The rethinking of the area would thus entail not only the architecture, but what architecture stands for and what the (changing) demands are for that now-empty area of Manhattan.

In-Stability

Our new model for downtown Manhattan was based on the idea that urban structures constantly evolve with global economical and political forces. The evolution of the last ten years of economic flux was studied and interpreted as consequences of growth to be extrapolated into a future "flex" program for the site. In fact, in a market where consistency and stability have given way to uncertainty and volatility, architecture would have to adapt to flexibility. Thus, the creation of our "Flex-City."

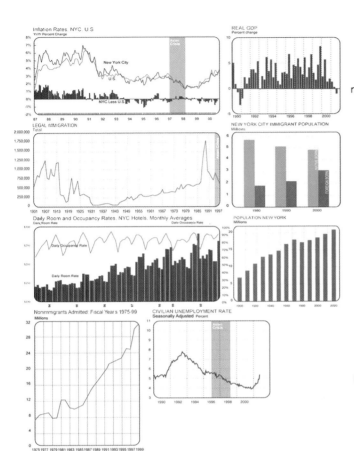

1990 - 2000 DATA FOR LOWER MANHATTAN

Populated mostly by people who want to live close as possible to their jobs: 88% are under 45, with 76% making over $90.000 a year, less than 10% have children under 18 | More than 56% of the city's population are foreign-born or the children of foreign-born | 2.3 millions were foreign-born and 5.2 millions native-born in 1990 | in 2000, 3.1 millions were foreign-born and 4.8 millions native-born | Population increase between 1990-2000 of 9.4% | in 2010 projected a continuationof that rate: population of 8.8 millions | Population density of 57 people per ha. |

MIKE BLOOMBERG / NYC Mayor / STATEMENT

Commercial: Zoning and economic development decisions must focus on mixed-use solutions | **Residential:** Increase the number of housing units by at least 100,000 |Encourage new residential uses in manufacturing districts | **Parks:** Our waterfront is a major asset | A community garden policy must be established | **Entertainment:** Establish a strong public education system and accessible health care | Generating $25 billion in revenue, Tourism is critical to the City|

2001 - 2010 EXTRAPOLATION OF FLEX-CITY

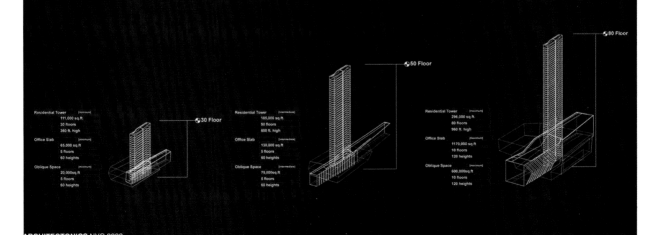

Generate

Flex-City is an interactive electronic environment where construction proposals are chosen, influenced, and ultimately created by the visitor. By selecting changes in certain logistic data (Econ Flex) and specific choice-driven data (Social Flex) one generates one of the eighty-one scenarios for downtown Manhattan. This interactive environment not only introduces new typologies for downtown Manhattan—horizontal slabs for office and commercial space, tall towers for apartments—but also specifically stresses "Flex Space," which distributes schools, medical units, and supermarkets, and "Green Flex," which introduces parks, tree-lined streets, and playgrounds. New infrastructures will add the necessary Flex-ability.

Integrate, Interact

Flex-City allows you to create a cityscape sensitive to Social Flex and Econ Flex. It combines constant instability (stock market and migration patterns) with permanent adjustment (local politics and tourist behavior). The Flex-archive will give you data and background information on the global flux of the last ten years; the extrapolation of these data indicates the prognosis for the next ten years. The flexibility will be found in the regeneration of a hybrid city model where mixed-use zones overlap and integrate in interlinked live-work-play-learn zones. Most variables are "exogenous," which means that one has to choose values for them on the basis of knowledge and intuition. For example, when circumstances change, people's behavior tends to change too. No forecast is solely based on hard data, the interpretation and extrapolation of human factors on these data are undeniable.

Hani Rashid is a leading figure in the fields of architectural design, digital interactive environments, and spatial experimentation. In 1988 he cofounded Asymptote, an award-winning design practice based in New York with partner Lisa Anne Couture. The work of Asymptote is in various museum collections including New York's Museum of Modern Art, the San Francisco Museum of Modern Art, the Canadian Center for Architecture, the Netherlands Institute of Architecture, and the Solomon R. Guggenheim Museum in New York City.

Asymptote

The Twin Twins

The World Trade Center towers as envisioned and designed by Minuro Yamasaki were not only formidable expressions of modernity and technological triumph, they were also monuments to the limitlessness of the human spirit. In creating a proposal for this site, we could bow to defeat and allow only ghosts or shadows of the great towers to remain in the place where they once stood, or we might take up the challenge to again build with the great confidence, vision, and courage that compelled the original towers. The World Trade Center ushered in the communications and information age and now, almost a half century later, the world has become a very different place, as has the human dimension of dreams and aspirations. The new Twin Twins, as envisioned, are not nostalgic ruminations for what no longer exists; rather they are a continuance and bifurcation of the formidable Yamasaki towers into entirely new entities that aspire to bring equal stature and power to the New York skyline of the twenty-first century.

    The Twin Twins at once recall and commemorate the vastness of what was lost by duplicating and reduplicating the Twin Towers' former presence. These new buildings are to be constructed of taut, technologically sophisticated surfaces: skins that express constant modulation and flux. Large openings in the massive undulating volumes accommodate sky gardens and large pools suspended high above the city. These penetrations of nature, light, and space infuse the building's interiors with air and natural light, while also providing places for observation, contemplation, and meditation. This proposal calls for vital working buildings for the digital age. Built on the traces of the elegant giants that preceded them, these are buildings that point the way to a vibrant and powerful future without resignation or apology.

Shigeru Ban was born in Tokyo in 1957. He attended the Southern California Institute of Architecture from 1977 to 1980 and continued his studies at Cooper Union School of Architecture, where he received his bachelor of architecture degree in 1984. Shigeru Ban established his private practice in Tokyo in 1985, and has since received the 1995 Mainichi Design Award, the 1997 JIA Prize for Best Young Architect of the Year, the 2000 Berlin Art Award, and the 2001 World Architecture Award.

Shigeru Ban

A Departure from the Ego

I designed this temporary World Trade Center Memorial immediately after September 11, without having been asked by anyone. Maybe I was motivated because of my experience of building the "Paper Church" after the Kobe earthquake of 1995. The church, built with the help of student volunteers, incorporated a structure made of paper tubes.

I cannot imagine designing another high-rise building to indicate "the EGO."

Carlos Brillembourg, AIA, is a registered architect and principal of Carlos Brillembourg Architects in New York. He received his M. Arch. degree in 1975 from Columbia University, and established his own practice in Caracas in 1980. Subsequently, he founded Carlos Brillembourg Architects in New York in 1984. His built work includes a theater, a sports center, office buildings, apartment buildings, a 250-room hotel, numerous single-family residences, and art galleries.

Carlos Brillembourg

A New Gateway for the City

This project acknowledges the catastrophic loss that occurred on September 11 and is at the same time a monument and a memorial. The Twin Towers were inseparable from the geography of the island. The towers functioned as a fundamental icon that transformed the geography and perception of New York City. Our proposal recognizes our responsibility to recuperate this monumental and symbolic presence.

We need to recall the utopian spirit of the original project. The buildings became a symbol of American capitalism, yet they were built by a government agency and did not make a profit until very recently. The towers were both a gateway into the city and a terminal that projected New York as a center of the global economy. The presence of the towers was ubiquitous, even in the most remote parts of the globe.

This project rebuilds the exact outline and location of the original towers and simultaneously opens up the core alternatively on the north–south and the east–west axes. This open space within the two towers creates a dialogue with the space in between. The perception of the towers from most directions will contain both the interior and exterior vertical space. The thin slabs of the new towers will increase the window perimeter of each building by 40 percent and will contain a mixture of office, commercial, and residential space. We feel strongly that subsidized housing should be given to the artists and writers who create the culture of New York.

New York has undergone a definitive change and this new condition allows us to rethink the entire project that inspired the original. The original, almost naive condition is permanently lost, but the shadow of the Twin Towers is forever cast on this site.

Mel Chin

Mel Chin is known for the broad range of approaches in his art, including works that require multidisciplinary, collaborative teamwork and works that conjoin cross-cultural aesthetics with complex ideas. Exhibited extensively throughout the United States and Europe, Chin is the recipient of many awards and grants, including a Cal Arts/Alpert Award, a Rockefeller Foundation grant, a Pollock/Krasner Foundation fellowship, a Tiffany Foundation Award, a Joan Mitchell Award, a Penny McCall Foundation Award, and multiple NEA fellowships.

Social Platform Readily Engaged in Active Development

Not a building, not a memorial.

> [I]nto the sky laying prone and vanquished in the embrace of the season
> of rain and death.
>
> —WILLIAM FAULKNER, *SANCTUARY*

A Boeing 767, full of fuel and the blood of innocents, arcing sharply in the blue sky over Manhattan on September 11, 2001, ended the reign of the skyscraper. Nuclear waste, bunker-busting bombs, and oxygen-depleting thermobaric explosives have made obsolete a shelter in use since the dawn of human existence—the cave.

The question is not which building to build to replace the shelters of the past but which direction to take in building for the future. As the destructive forces of terrorism and war provoke the military imagination toward more horrific inventions, what does the creative individual or team produce in the wake of such events? As Bertolt Brecht noted to Walter Benjamin, "Do not build on the good old days but on the bad new ones."

Rising from lines of ash, debris, and death drawn by FEMA as its boundaries, horizontally spreading across lower Manhattan, skirting open spaces and parks and subsiding before Ground Zero, leaving it time and space to find its recovery, is a new system resting in the old canyons of late modernism.

S.P.R.E.A.D. (Social Platform Readily Engaged in Active Development) is a modular platform, suspended seventy-two feet above the streets and avenues of downtown New York City. It is a grid of new material combinations, filled with fibers and fluids of data, water, and power, and capable of generating new acres of sustainable infrastructure. This platform, managing its own wastes and water, equipped with an undercarriage of light, is buoyed by its skyscraper neighbors in symbiotic attachment. In exchange for structural support, it can supply its hosts additional power and water conservation as well as portals into new work and leisure spaces.

A "system," as opposed to a building, is proposed as a response to the destroyed World Trade Center. This New World Trade City is new acreage for New Yorkers, a horizontal plane supporting single-story offices and "green park" components built on "floating" foundations. These work/green spaces can move about on a grid (not unlike the cars and trucks below) arranging, connecting, and adapting to the needs and desires of people who work and play within, above and below.

A massive, object-based, monolithic expression of individual design has tragically fallen. Rising in its place is S.P.R.E.A.D. It responds to the presence of a multitude of sites needing a new generation of designers to provide a diverse new city of human-scaled shelters, in an unusual open space.

A massive, ever-changing, adaptable infrastructure that teems with a life of creative talent responding to the diversity of human needs is a fitting response to the destruction of terror and war.

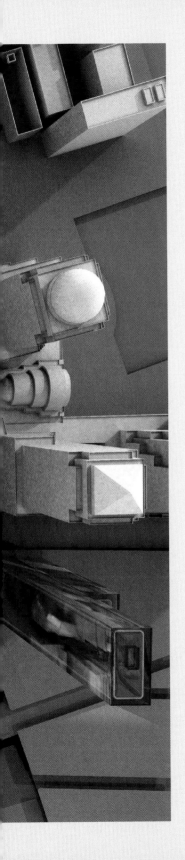

Preston Scott Cohen is a professor of architecture at Harvard Design School. He is the author of *Contested Symmetries and Other Predicaments in Architecture* (Princeton Architectural Press, 2001). Cohen's work has been widely exhibited and published. K+D Lab, Dean Di Simone and Joseph Kosinski, principles with Chris Hoxie, is a digital, architectural, broadcast and web design firm whose work has been exhibited and published widely.

Preston Scott Cohen with K+D Lab

Thin Towers

The aftermath of the World Trade Center disaster yields one of those rare occasions when an urban design is compelled to resynthesize disparate civic and proprietary interests by means of anomalous spaces and arrangements. In other words, in this case, urban design becomes architecture.

The exceptional situation demands an unusual combination of three elements: a memorial for the "cemetery without graves," an urban park, and commercial space. The proposal fulfills a number of different desires: it creates a new skyline and a complex combination of office, residential, retail, recreational, contemplative, and commemorative programs, and reestablishes continuity with the fabric of the city and with its rhythms of life.

The streets of the financial district extend into an open green space linked to Battery Park City. Pedestrian streets pass over the submerged west side highway. The skewed north–south streets establish view corridors in which to locate towers as fixed points of reference within the new site. The memorial will derive its specificity from the need to commemorate the individuals who died rather than from a triumphant national response. The vastness of this site alone, as well as its length, make it an exception among the important civic spaces of the city. Permanent markers, makeshift shrines, and figurative sculptures dedicated to the collective rescue effort will take their place on the block's elevated floor. Near the new towers, pavers indicate the locations of the former twin towers. But life goes on among the traces of past places and tragic events.

The reintroduction of skyscrapers poses the most conspicuous problem. In view of the inevitable association of this site with collective fear and devastation, it becomes extremely difficult, if not downright impossible, to propose towers comparable in dimensions to the Twin Towers. We must then admit, perhaps, that the context would benefit from a less monolithic configuration. How then can smaller towers coexist with the memory of the Ground Zero site zone, accommodate the memorial, leave the open space necessary to the revitalization of pedestrian activity, and contain sufficient leasable space to recover a significant percentage of the space lost?

The solution is a radical reduction of tower floor plate area relative to tower height. The new towers are exceedingly thin relative to their height. This allows them to remain as unobtrusive as possible at the ground. The height of buildings is assessed not only by actual and apparent dimensions, but also by relative proportions. Vertically attenuated and staggered in plan, the proposed towers appear from afar to be closer together, taller, and perhaps farther away than they actually are. The manifestation of this illusion also bears on the problem of how to accommodate greater volume and hence viable office space in certain towers, as opposed to hotel and residential programs in others; for the office towers, flanking buildings are attached that appear to leave the formal integrity of the taller pieces intact.

Motivated by the peculiar imperative to reconsider a skyline after the disappearance of one of its preeminent icons, the thin towers establish the skyline itself as a definitive form rather than reestablishing a singular discernible icon. Insofar as New York is fundamentally a city of skyscrapers, it was built upon speculations that exceeded expectations and precedents. Now we have to stimulate the imagination to greater heights without resorting to conspicuous forms of gigantism. Proportions supplant dimensions.

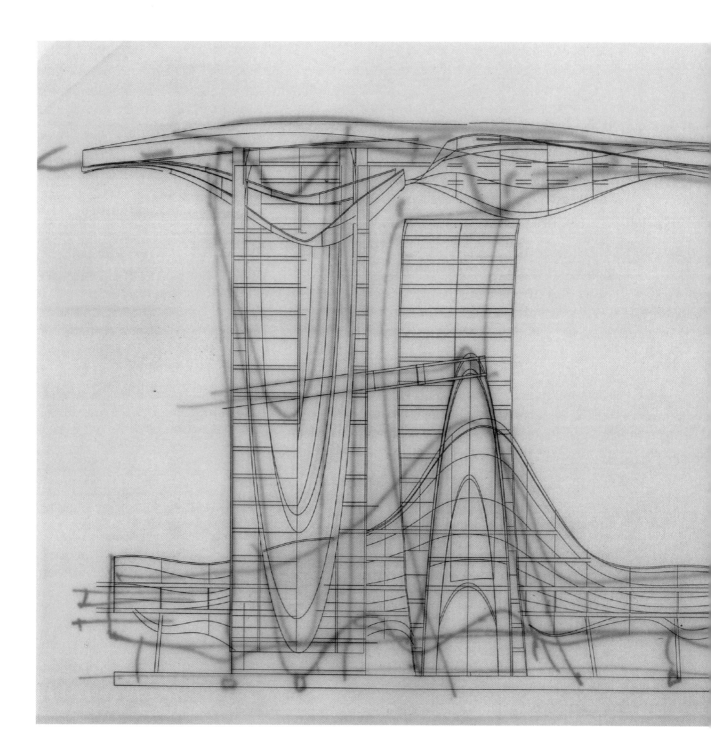

Coop Himmelb(l)au was founded in 1968 in Vienna, Austria, by Wolf D. Prix and Helmut Swiczinsky and has since then continued to work within the fields of urbanism, architecture, design, and art. In 1988 and 2000 second offices were opened in Los Angeles, California, and Guadalajara, Mexico, respectively. Coop Himmelb(l)au has realized projects ranging from remodeling in Vienna to city planning in France. The most widely recognized projects include the Rooftop Remodeling in Vienna, Austria, the master plan for the city of Melun-Sénart in France, the Museum Pavilion in Groningen, Netherlands, and the UFA-Cinema Center, a multifunctional cinema complex in Dresden.

Coop Himmelb(l)au

The Tower of Babel Revisited

Reversed towers, built upside down, will provide multifunctional cultural signs for the future of architecture. New forms, technologies, and contents will create a renewed urban focus that is not concerned with the past but looks forward into an optimistic future.

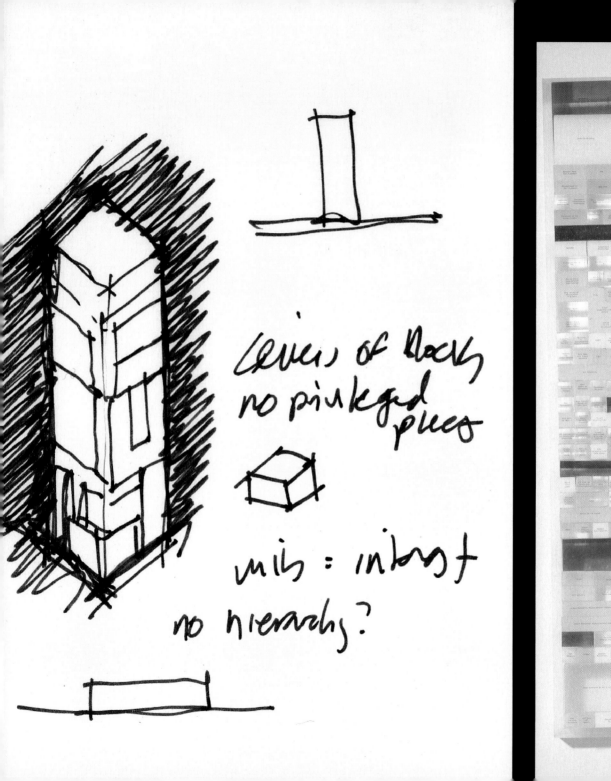

Levels of blocks
no privileged
place

mix = interest

no hierarchy?

Jared Della Valle was born in New York City in 1971. He received his bachelor of arts degree from Lehigh University and completed degrees in architecture and construction management from Washington University in St. Louis. Andrew Bernheimer was born in Boston, Massachusetts, in 1968. He received his bachelor of arts degree from Williams College and his master's degree in architecture from Washington University. Della Valle + Bernheimer Design was founded in 1996. The firm has completed diverse design work, including residential, commercial, and public projects. They were selected as winners of the first San Francisco Prize in Architecture and the Architectural League of New York's 2002 Young Architects Forum.

Della Valle + Bernheimer Design

Castle Building

We are concerned that the rush to rebuild downtown Manhattan will preclude reasoned and sensitive development. Over the last four months, various people and special interest groups have demanded a voice in the regeneration of downtown Manhattan. In that time, the difficulty of orchestrating dialogue between these often-competing groups has become clear. But such dialogue is necessary before any new construction begins.

Our project proposes a device for the study of currently indeterminate relationships. We have identified eighty groups that will have a hand in helping shape the new downtown. To these groups we have assigned a numerical and volumetric value based on our perception of their influence on the future of this project. A block, built in scale to this assigned value and colored or textured based on interest group, represents each entity: frosted acrylic blocks correspond to public-sector entities, clear acrylic blocks correspond to design, planning, and advocacy groups, white acrylic blocks correspond to private-sector interests, and colored acrylic blocks correspond to significant emotions that we have internally identified as catalysts of the site redesign process.

The assemblage of blocks can be arranged and rearranged endlessly. A physical metaphor for the complex dialogue required by the task of rebuilding, it illustrates the dynamic of power and influence at play in the redevelopment effort. This bracing model only reinforces our conviction that the programming and redesign of downtown Manhattan should be an open, communal, and democratic process.

Field Operations was created in 2000 by urban designer and landscape architect James Corner in partnership with architect Stan Allen. The mandate of the firm is to provide innovative, high-quality design solutions for urban sites and public spaces. Recently, Field Operations has been recognized with first prize in the Fresh Kills Landfill to Landscape International Design Competition and the prestigious Daimler-Chrysler Design Award for innovative design, 2000.

Field Operations

A Memorial at Fresh Kills

Less visible than the massive Ground Zero site in lower Manhattan, an equally important recovery effort took place at Fresh Kills, Staten Island. Working on top of newly sealed earth mounds, a team of investigators sorted millions of tons of debris in their search for traces of the missing. The city has suffered a violent displacement. This austere site in Staten Island is the final resting place of the World Trade Center's ruins.

To honor the dead of September 11, the labors of the recovery workers, and especially the firefighters and police officers of Staten Island, we have proposed a processional earthwork on landfill mound one of nine at Fresh Kills. This immense monument sits alone in an expansive wildflower prairie. Its two earthforms mirror the exact width and height of the towers, and its second incline is on axis with the skyline vista where the towers once stood. As visitors ascend, they will pass small inset markers commemorating the dead and missing at each floor.

Other memorials can and should be constructed, both on Staten Island and at Ground Zero. With this proposal, we simply want to mark the site of the recovery effort at Fresh Kills, and to provide a large simple space, open to the sky and the distant horizon, where the visitor can find a place for quiet reflection. This proposal forms an integral part of a larger transformation of Fresh Kills from landfill to a vast new urban park and nature preserve.

Established in 1993 by Farshid Moussavi and Alejandro Zaera-Polo, Foreign Office Architects brings an innovative approach to the integration of landscape and buildings. The practice is completing an impressive ferry terminal with landscaped public areas and cruise liner facilities at the heart of Yokohama Bay in Japan while constructing a number of other commissions in Spain, Korea, and Holland. The practice is also known recently for its highly acclaimed restaurant designs for the Belgo chain in London and New York.

Foreign Office Architects

The World's Tallest Building Back in New York

We have a great site in a great city and the opportunity to have the world's tallest building back in New York. Ground Zero used to host 1.3 million square meters of workspace, and that is a good size to attempt to return to New York its legitimate possession.

The Bundle-Tower: A New High-Rise Prototype

The world's tallest building requires a new high-rise typology. The evolution of the skyscraper type is a process in which the increase in height of the building makes it necessary to concentrate the structure in the periphery of the plan. As the lateral forces become stronger than the gravitational ones, it becomes necessary to maximize the structure's moment of inertia. But as the structure grows taller, the slenderness of the organization reaches the limit and the depth of the plan needs to increase proportionally. In order to generate a new type of high-rise, our proposal is to operate with the building massing, rather than with just the distribution of the structure. Our proposal is to form the complex as a bundle of interconnected towers that buttress each other structurally, increasing the structure's moment of inertia without necessarily increasing the floor depth or the total area.

Total footprint 8000 Sqm

35m

Bundle Scale and Number

The average rental workspace floor size in New York City is one thousand square meters, and we have taken that as our quantum, or bundle scale, in the new WTC. As our target is to reach approximately five hundred meters high, we are aiming at approximately 110 floors with a conventional floor-to-floor height of 4.5 meters. If we take the size of the former complex as a measure of total floor size, we have:

$$\frac{884{,}000 \text{ square meters}}{110 \text{ floors}} = 8036 \text{ square meters per floor}$$

This equals approximately eight towers of one thousand square meters per floor.

Isomorphic Tubular Structure

In order to maximize the ratio between floor area and perimeter, and to improve the structural performance of the building, we have opted for a tubular structural lattice on the facade of circular towers. The tubes bend vertically to buttress each other approximately every 165 meters. The lattice of the tower structure and the geometry of the bunch tower are self-similar structures.

Elevator System and Transfer Lobbies: A Network of Vertical Circulations

Every tower, with an approximate area of 110,000 square meters, will be provided with a battery of twelve high-speed elevators that will provide access primarily to the floors in the tower, but will form part of a network of sky lobbies that every tower shares with the two neighboring ones every thirty-six floors. The fire escape systems, HVAC, and fire-suppression, electricity, and telecommunications systems are also contained in this network of vertical cores.

Variable-Depth and Variable-Area Floor Space

As the vertical structure is always concentrated in the periphery of the tubes, the slabs inside the towers are column-free circles of thirty-six-meter diameter. The vertical circulation core remains vertical, providing a periodical variation in the depth of workspace between the bending envelope and the core.

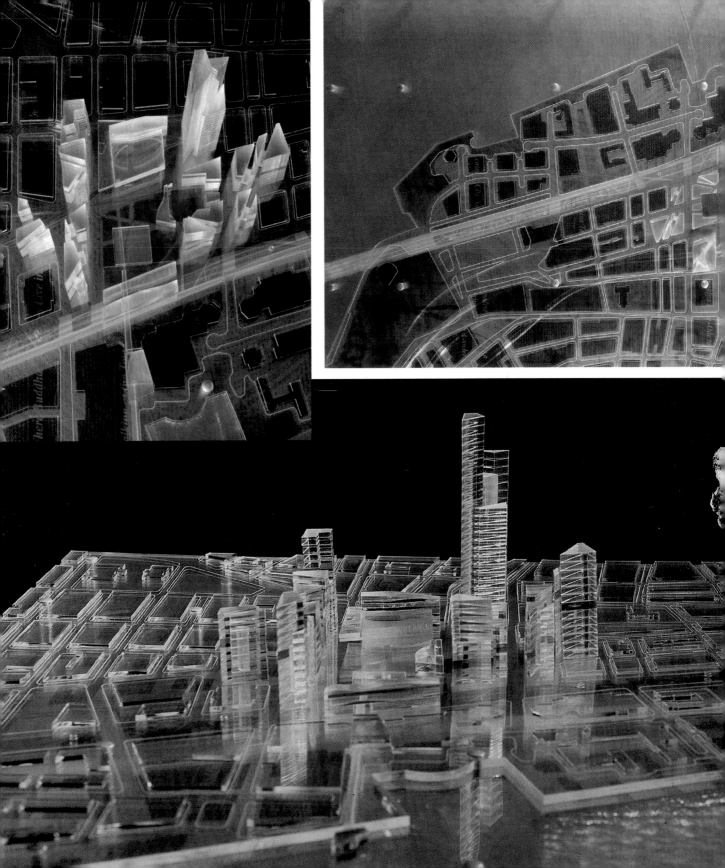

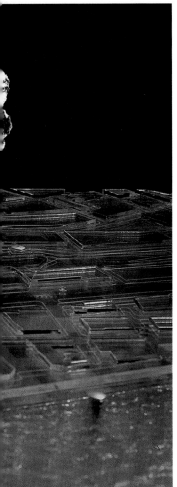

Fox & Fowle Architects is one of New York's leading design firms. Founded in 1978, the practice has grown to include office buildings, educational facilities, museums, transportation centers, and master plans. The firm's design reputation is further enhanced by its commitment to sustainable design and its experience creating high-performance buildings. Daniel Kaplan is principal-in-charge of the firm's award-winning High-Rise Studio. He has served in a design and leadership capacity for the firm's largest projects.

Fox & Fowle

A New Urban Precinct

This layered construction answers the obligation to build an exemplary urban precinct—with world-class public space, infrastructure, and architecture—that embodies the highest aspirations for the future of New York City.

The new precinct, unlike its predecessor, is connected to the two adjacent city street grids: the organic downtown pattern and the orthogonal uptown grid. It is linked to the balance of the city and the region beyond by a new transportation hub—a "Grand Central Station" for downtown Manhattan. A new linear park, located at grade level above a newly buried West Street, serves as a connector between the nineteenth-century city edge and Battery Park City.

A matrix of thirty-to-forty-story, multiuse loft blocks forms the northern and southern edges of a grand new urban space. These blocks are shot through with an angular skein of public and semipublic spaces, establishing a network of human-scale connections. An eighty-story fissured tower takes its place in the company of downtown's tallest spires.

A contemporary art museum occupies the critical hinge between large-scale east–west and north–south spaces. Public circulation on both axes intersects and intertwines with the internal program. A second group of cultural buildings clusters around a semienclosed public space. These will serve as the locus of memorial and interpretative functions.

The twin footprints of the towers are left as voids, as hallowed ground. They exist in uneasy balance as places of silence within the new, vibrant, and dense city pattern.

Joseph Giovannini is a principal of Giovannini Architecture, a design firm in New York and Los Angeles. A Pulitzer Prize nominee, he has been an architecture critic for the *Los Angeles Herald Examiner* and the *New York Times,* and has written for numerous international publications. Giovannini received a bachelor of arts in English literature from Yale University, a master of arts in French language and literature at the Sorbonne, and a master of architecture degree from the Graduate School of Design at Harvard University. Rodrigo Monsalve, Chilean born, has worked in architecture in Europe and the United States. He lived for five years in the rain forest of Patagonia researching architectural theory. In 1996 he met Joseph Giovannini. Their architectural design collaborations have been internationally published. Monsalve's design experience includes applied concepts of Renaissance painting and twentieth-century Constructivist plastic arts in contemporary residential and commercial architecture.

Joseph Giovannini & Rodrigo Monsalve

Two Pools, Two Voids

Proposal: The Hudson breaches the retaining walls surrounding the Twin Towers, flooding the two footprints from which the buildings once soared, the planes of water rising and falling with the estuarial tides in pools of remembrance. The surface is placid but at the same time disturbed. Set in utterly simple, flat granite decks that tilt imperceptibly, the water itself appears to slope in a subtle optical illusion: the pools that reflect the sky are serene but troubled, elemental but unnatural. The water acts as a lens magnifying shards of reflective stainless steel at the bottom of the pools, memories of violence now smoothed over by waters of time in an urban subconscious.

The two footprints of the Twin Towers are proposed as dedicated memorials, with the names of the three thousand dead inscribed in glass walls that retain the water and rise up from the angled ground allowing water to spill over the names. The rest of the site, about ten acres, will be rebuilt with porous blocks of buildings dedicated to a mixture of uses typical of New York's urban delirium. The square footage lost on September 11 is rebuilt here in a collar ringing the angular street patterns typical of downtown. These complex, fractal geometries form the basis of a fragmented architecture that attempts to correct by example the monolithic simplicity that once removed the Twin Towers from the pedestrian fabric of the city. Still, within the collar of buildings, the Twin Towers are embedded as voids running the height of the new buildings, forming a hollow above huge vertical courtyards that remember the towers while giving light, air, and space to the new structures. Buildings that once seemed indestructible solids have turned into tall voids, existing as absences within the new buildings. Visitors can walk into these courts, which open at grade to the surrounding streets, and see facades replicated from the downed towers. They are living, working facades, but haunted.

Gluckman Mayner Architects is the successor firm to Richard Gluckman Architects, which was established in 1977. The firm has designed a wide range of institutional, commercial, and residential projects throughout the United States, Europe, and Asia, establishing a distinctive reputation for its rigorous approach to the design and construction of architecture of every scale, particularly buildings of national and international cultural importance.

Gluckman Mayner Architects

Towers for the Twenty-First Century

Our suggestion for the New World Trade Center consists of rebuilding the towers to conform to the original profiles. The skin of the new building, however, should reflect a response to the nature of the September 11 tragedy. We endeavor to explore the multitude of possibilities of glass and electronic media and the potential results when they are integrated in sensitive or operable skin. Electrochromatic glass, for example, can allow the building's skin to change colors and transform from opaque to clear. On the other hand, interlaced lenticular screens and holography will make this transformation alive and interactive as one passes around the buildings. By means of glow and abstraction, the skin can express different emotions. The new skin of light will enclose an enormous void that will be filled by new programmatic parameters. They will include cultural, residential, commercial, public, and civic spaces, as well as recreational and memorial spaces.

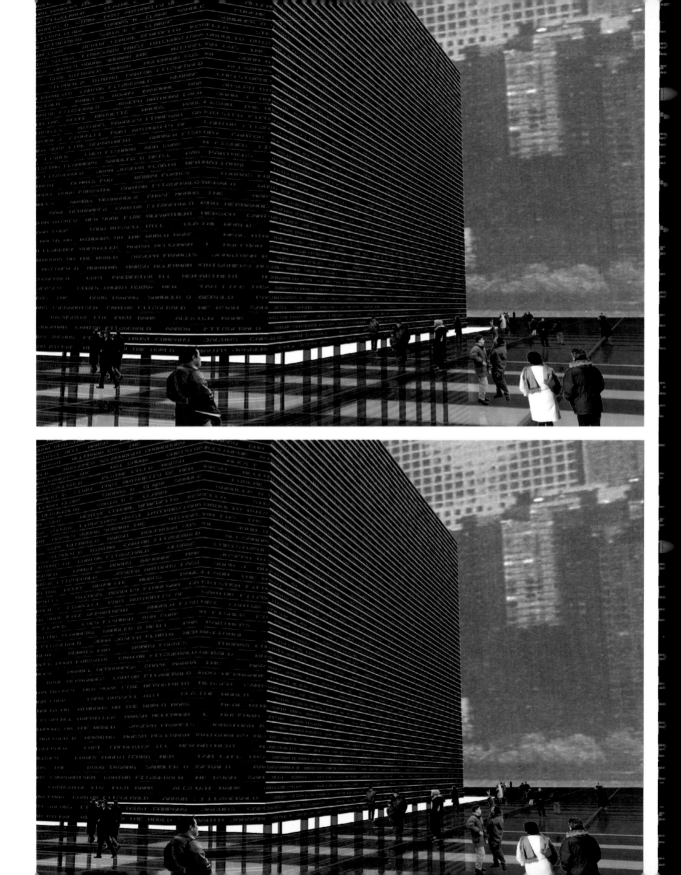

Alexander Gorlin established his architectural practice in 1987 after returning from a Rome Prize Fellowship at the American Academy in Rome. Gorlin holds degrees from the Cooper Union School of Architecture and the Yale School of Architecture. Brendan Cotter is a graduate of the Princeton University Graduate School of Architecture. He is presently senior associate at Alexander Gorlin Architects. Cotter has taught at the Princeton University School of Architecture. The firm has won two AIA Design Awards.

Alexander Gorlin Architects

The Dream of Vishnu

When the towers collapsed into dust, it recalled the Hindu concept of the world as illusion, the reality that we know, a dream in the mind of Vishnu, one of the triumvirate rulers of the universe. What was apparently a most solid and permanent part of the city—the two towers of concrete and steel—dissolved and melted before the eyes of millions both in person and on the television screen. All at once, buildings and life are seen as equally ephemeral. To commemorate the tragic murder of thousands at the World Trade Center, the entire site is to be dedicated as a memorial to the death of innocent civilians and uniformed personnel. The 110 stories of the two towers are literally compressed into 110 feet, creating two monoliths of the same footprint inscribed with the names of all the victims. The names are on a liquid crystal display, moving endlessly around the two blocks, whose proportions recall the mastaba tombs of ancient Egypt. The electronic display re-creates the idea of the names in a form that highlights the evanescent nature of both life and architecture: indeed, the events of September 11, 2001, prove that life and art are short. In contrast to the names that are commemorated above, visible below the horizontal glass plane is the archaeology of the ruins of the site, from the foundations of the Twin Towers to the subway and train lines that ran beneath. The hellish destruction is left as a sign, a record of the evil act that should not be forgotten, so that it should never happen again.

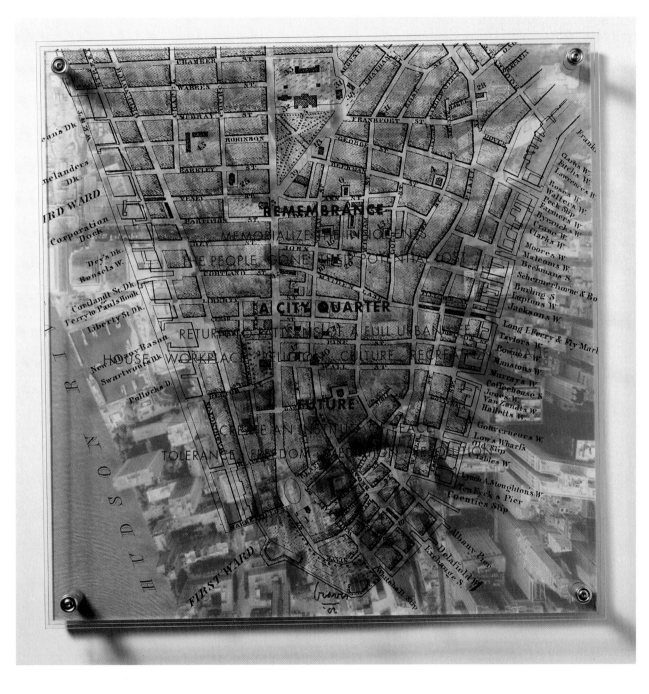

Michael Graves founded his practice in 1964 in Princeton, New Jersey. His projects all over the world have directly influenced the transformation of urban architecture from abstract modernism toward more contextual and traditional themes. A native of Indianapolis, Graves received his architectural training at the University of Cincinnati and Harvard University.

Michael Graves & Associates

A Restored Urban Context

We can never erase the memory of the tragic events of September 11, which will without a doubt require a central formal monument of some kind, whose form is as yet unknown to us. I feel, however, that the most meaningful way to memorialize the innocent victims and their lost potential would be a marker within a restored context of layered urban pattern on the site.

Vitality in urban life results from a mix of activities—public and private, daytime and nighttime, residential and commercial. The vitality of those we lost can thus be reflected in this revitalized area of our damaged city. Within an infrastructure of cultural, recreational, educational, and religious pursuits could be found a place for institutions that address issues of tolerance and freedom worldwide. This would be part of the forward-looking, positive approach with which one would develop the project.

I envision the rebuilt site much like a traditional city quarter, as shown symbolically in a layer of this exhibition piece that is a historic map of New York. This development would be of a density appropriate to the Manhattan of today.

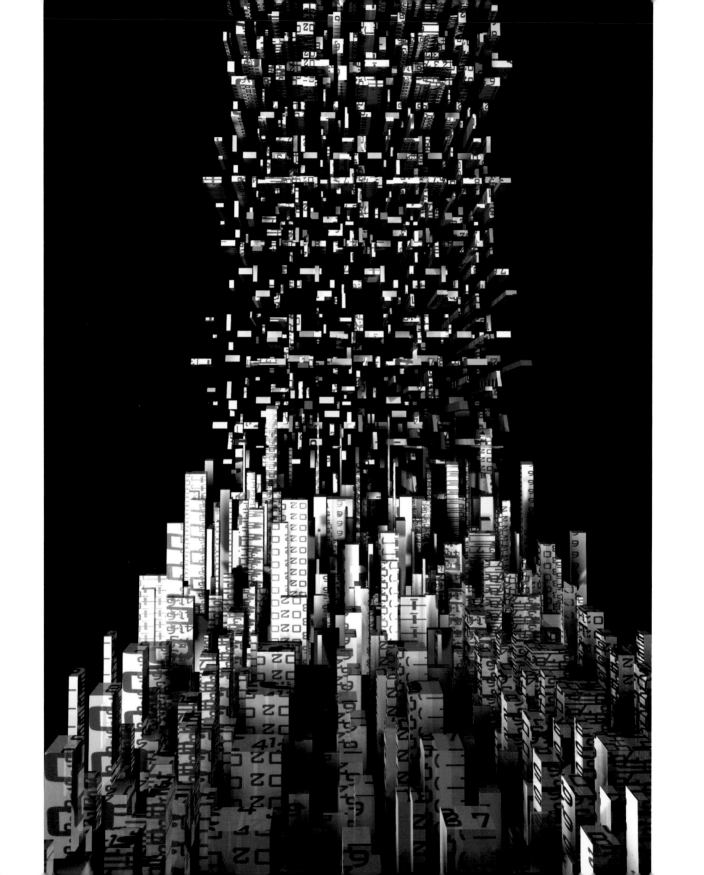

Zaha Hadid is an architect who consistently pushes the boundaries of architecture and urban design. Her work experiments with spatial quality, extending and intensifying existing landscapes in the pursuit of a visionary aesthetic that encompasses all fields of design, ranging from urban scale through to products, interiors, and furniture. She is best known for her seminal built works, though her central concerns involve a simultaneous engagement in practice, teaching, and research.

Zaha Hadid

From Destructive Impact to Creative Impulse

The tragic destruction of the World Trade Center raises the question of what could replace it. Rather than calling for a symbolic response, the question is what kind of organizational structure would satisfy contemporary business life and what kind of formal language would articulate it? What are the functionality and aesthetics of the contemporary metropolis? How, if at all, should its essence be reflected in the Manhattan skyline?

The World Trade Center was one of the largest and most ambitious structures ever built. Minoru Yamasaki designed this complex, comprising the Twin Towers plus five lower buildings, in the mid- to late sixties. This was at the peak of the era of Fordism, the system of assembly-line mass production that led to modern mass society organized around huge corporations. The World Trade Center was one of the culminating investments of the long postwar boom. Construction of the towers started in 1969 and was completed in 1973. The Twin Towers alone offered one million square meters of office space spread over 110 stories. The total center offered working space for fifty thousand people, equivalent to the population of a medium-sized city.

Fordism in general was marked by massive endeavors. Everything was produced in bulk quantities and everything was based on standardization and reproduction: grids, series, and the repetition of the same! Yamasaki's Twin Towers developed this principle to its ultimate symbolic conclusion: even such an enormous, iconic structure as the great American skyscraper could be subordinated to

the principle of repetition. The repetition of the same operated between the two towers as well as within each tower.

The epoch of the skyscraper is over, not primarily because of concerns for security, but because the skyscraper's organizational structure is too simple and too constricting. A tower only grows in one dimension. The strict linearity of its extension accounts for its characteristic poverty of connectivity. Towers are hermetic units, which are themselves arrays of equally hermetic units (floors). These features of linearity and strict segmentation are antithetical to contemporary business relations as well as to contemporary urban life in general. Much higher levels of complexity are required to spatially order and articulate contemporary relations.

The demise of Fordism and of the skyscraper as its urban archetype does not imply the retreat from the large scale nor from high density. Both bigness and density are increasing within the contemporary metropolis.

The exhaustion of the historic city centers—there are simply not enough of them to satisfy the insatiable need for contemporary urbanity—and the bankruptcy of comprehensive city planning in the face of market uncertainty mean that architecture has to carry the burden of urbanism within large single developments. Architecture has been mostly overburdened with this task. However, new spatial models should be able to organize higher levels of complexity and integrate significantly more simultaneous programmatic agendas and diverse life processes. But how can appropriate spatial patterns be invented and how can the required spatial complexity be built up? The task is to devise strategies that can produce large buildings that fulfill the function of urban communication and exchange.

We will project an entity of a higher order than what one usually considers as "building" or even "ensemble," an entity that re-creates within itself approximations of the multiplicity, complexity, and effectiveness of the urban: a city compressed into a large building. The time factor is also to be introduced in scenarios of phasing and reconfiguration. We believe that the large components of the contemporary metropolis have to be conceived as evolving rather than finished and fixed structures.

We should tackle this significant site only after we have gathered sufficient intellectual and creative resources—in other words, after we are satisfied that our intervention has a chance to articulate the essential operations and ambitions of the contemporary metropolis with the same poignancy and profundity that made the World Trade Center such an effective symbol of modern civilization. Approaching the task in this spirit opens up the opportunity to realize a large-scale urban intervention with a significant transformative impulse for the whole of Manhattan.

Hugh Hardy, FAIA, founded the interdisciplinary architecture and planning firm Hardy Holzman Pfeiffer Associates in 1967. His New York portfolio includes restoration and reconstruction, high-rise buildings, urban renewal, and restaurants. Born in 1932, Mr. Hardy earned his bachelor of arts degree and master's degree in architecture from Princeton. In 1962, after serving in the Army Corps of Engineers, he established Hugh Hardy & Associates, precursor to HHPA, which now has projects all over America and in countries as distant as New Zealand and Singapore.

Hugh Hardy

Manhattan Redux

The profile of lower Manhattan seen from the harbor has long been a symbol of New York City. Its pinnacled shafts once offered a landmark view to arriving ocean liners, identifying this as a place of towering ambition and accomplishment. It all changed in the 1960s as new, boxy buildings were made, climaxing with the twin World Trade Center towers. These two flat-topped extrusions dominated the skyline until 2001. Despite their prominence, they were alien impositions without human scale, lacking compatibility with their neighbors. But we became used to their presence, and without them the city's profile seems tentative and indistinct. The remaining boxy buildings loom larger, muscling out the romantic shapes of an earlier generation. Now that we have an opportunity to build anew, surely lower Manhattan can become a better place to live and work, with fanciful varied buildings of many configurations. The water can be our transport, view, and playground. We can create a new city here by enhancing what is already in place. We can join the built with the natural landscape, lifting them into the air and celebrating New York as a city built on water.

Gisue and Mojgan Hariri, Iranian-born, Cornell-educated sisters, opened their New York City practice, Hariri & Hariri, in 1986. High style, handicraft, a sense of place, and social agendas coexist in their work, which emphasizes use of materials and an understanding of pure light and space. Their Digital-House was part of the *Un-Private House* exhibition at the Museum of Modern Art in 1999, and was chosen as a finalist for the Saatchi & Saatchi Innovation in Communication Award in 2000.

Hariri & Hariri

The Weeping Towers

We propose that the whole site be a memorial with an evolving structure composed of eleven weeping towers. These towers symbolically represent the heroic scale of the Twin Towers, but serve only as vertical circulation to observation decks, also providing mechanical, electrical and digital cores for the future structures to come. We envision "free-form" buildings hovering above the earth and bridging between these towers. These structures would be for a state-of-the-art New York Stock Exchange and a World Culture Museum. Reaching between the towers and floating in the sky, these structures will be visible to the entire city, signifying the heart and the strength of our freedom and the world's financial capital.

The exterior of the towers will be wrapped in a "smart skin," where information and data can be displayed both to the occupants inside and the visitors on the outside, with a device detecting potential objects approaching the site. The skin would also be equipped with a sprinkler system and a device transmitting mist, allowing the architecture to participate in the memory of this tragedy and weep.

Additionally, we propose an annual event, to be held on September 11, as a global day of mourning and gathering, a day when people come together at the site to mourn and simply be with one another. On this day the eleven "Weeping Towers" will transmit a mist from their skin, allowing the architecture to participate in the event, offering a deep ceremony, intensely personal and emotionally powerful.

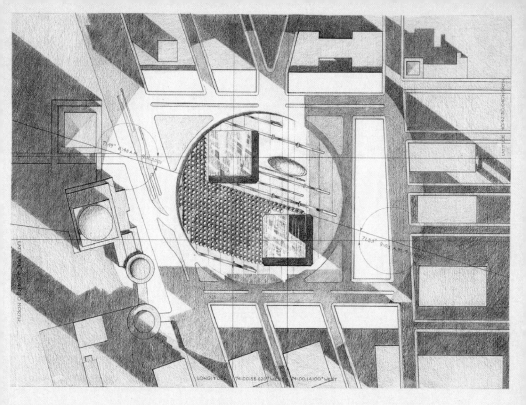

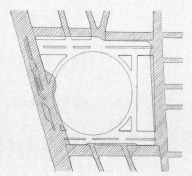

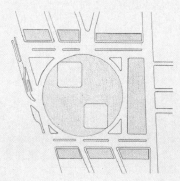

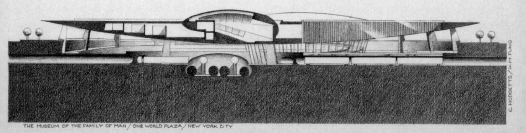

THE MUSEUM OF THE FAMILY OF MAN / ONE WORLD PLAZA / NEW YORK CITY

C. HODGETTS / H. M. FUNG

Hodgetts + Fung Design Associates, the firm of Craig Hodgetts and Hsin-Ming Fung, is noted for its ability to realize artistically challenging projects while respecting the constraints of time, practice, and economic reality. Their work is technically adventurous and deeply embedded in context, reflecting their view that architecture exists in the moment as well as the mind.

Hodgetts + Fung Design Associates

The Museum of the Family of Man

It has now become clear that the cultural diversity which has come to be the hallmark of a free society is not fairly represented in the museums and institutions which attempt to paint a formal portrait of man's role here on earth. We believe this is the time and the place to establish an institution that is dedicated to all the world's people. In it, we would hope to find records of those elements that define our collective culture, that define differences, and that are defined by belief. The Museum of the Family of Man that we propose ought to be an autonomous entity, beholden to no one, yet committed to each soul that has taken a breath.

One World Plaza

We believe it is most important to commemorate the conscience of the world's people by dedicating the space formerly occupied by the World Trade Center to the cause of peace and harmony, and suggest the creation of One World Plaza. This plaza should be devoted, in all aspects, to the belief in our family, the family of man, and to the appreciation and support of the variations to be found in our lives, cultures, habits, and beliefs. A vast circular lawn, over six hundred feet in diameter, will offer space for contemplation and reflection, and two pools will recall the positions of the Twin Towers. A grove in the form of the shadows cast by the towers at the time of the tragedy will form a memorial for those who perished in the attack.

New Construction

A plaza can be created in a manner which honors the sanctity of the site, yet provides for development opportunities to restore economic vitality to the area by reconfiguring the street grid to provide new construction sites on the periphery of the plaza. Use of the right of way of the streets bordering the World Trade Center as sites for new construction will provide eight to ten million square feet of new office space, which will frame the plaza.

Conclusion

It is our hope that this project will help to direct discussion of the issues surrounding the September 11 tragedy toward a living memorial to those who lost their lives, a memorial which restores confidence in the basic goodness of our kind and helps us as individuals and as a nation to further our understanding of those with whom we share the earth.

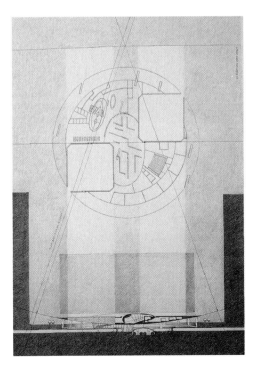

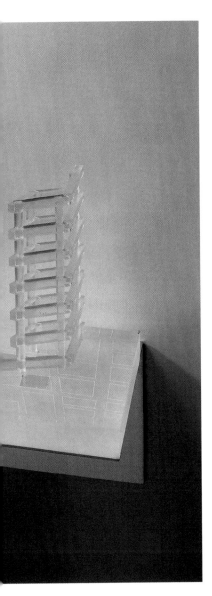

Steven Holl established Steven Holl Architects in New York in 1976. Holl is an honors graduate of the University of Washington. He studied architecture in Rome in 1970, and did postgraduate work at the Architectural Association in London in 1976. His firm was awarded the winning design among 516 entries in the competition for the new Museum of Contemporary Art, Helsinki, which opened to the public in May 1998. Among his most recent honors are the 1996 Progressive Architecture Awards for Excellence in Design for the Knut Hamsun Museum in Bødo, Norway, and the Museum of the City in Cassina, Italy. In 1989 the Museum of Modern Art featured Holl's work in a two-person exhibition.

Steven Holl

Floating Memorial/Folded Street

> Only a very small part of architecture belongs to art: the tomb and the monument.
>
> —ADOLF LOOS

The project is an enormous series of spaces for reflection. Light enters through the gaps between blackened concrete walls. One long chamber contains the photographs of each person who perished. These photos of their faces are laid horizontally with inch-thick glass set into concrete. There is a recessed holder below each photo for a candle. When the sun goes down these candles provide the light. As the World Trade Center tragedy took many souls without bodies to bury (no ground), this monumental space "floats," with the river water moving below.

The memorial ramps up to a new bridge over West Street, connected to a "folded street" which ascends over the site. Along the ascending "street" are a number of functions: galleries, cinema spaces, cafés, restaurants, a hotel, classrooms for a branch of New York University. Sheathed in translucent glass, the truss construction allows for grand public observation decks. A new street-level plan allows north–south and east–west streets to go through the site while accommodating various new functions, such as auditorium halls with large capacities. Footprints of the original towers are formed into 212-foot-by-212-foot reflective ponds, with glass lenses allowing light to enter the spaces below.

Born in 1934, Austrian architect, planner, designer, teacher, writer, and artist Hans Hollein has completed projects and won competitions internationally, including the Museum of Modern Art in Frankfurt and the General/Media Tower in Vienna. Awarded the prestigious Pritzker Architecture Prize in 1985, Hollein, whose architectural and artistic works are in renowned museums around the globe, is recognized as one of the world's leading architects.

Hans Hollein

A Dynamic Piece of Memory

The new World Trade Center should, as a sign of continuity in spite of aggression and destruction, recall the old World Trade Center, but with the significant addition of a dynamic piece of memory. I therefore propose to reerect the two towers in basically the same shape and height and to connect them on top with a hovering object whose role is that of a memorial to September 11, housing an information center on the state of the global fight against terrorism, a tribute to all victims worldwide, an area for a dialogue on tolerance, and a space for meditation. Spatially and urbanistically this is a proposal founded on some of my ideas on Manhattan of the early sixties, suggesting a horizontal extension of the city above the verticality of the high-rise, a commanding gesture of the eternal spirit of men.

Man has always built for survival, survival during life and survival after life.

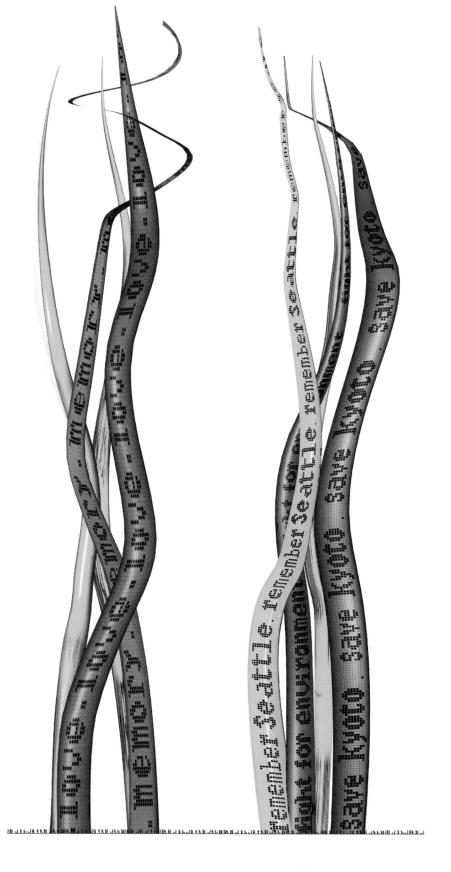

Jakob + MacFarlane's work is created from a series of ongoing investigations, motivated directly by an interest in specificity. Recent work explores digital technology as both a conceptual and fabrication means, using new materials to create a more flexible, responsive, immediate environment. Major projects include the restaurant Georges at the Centre Georges Pompidou, Paris (2000), the reconstruction of the Theatre of Pont-Audemer, France (1999–2000), and the Communication Center for Renault in Paris (2003).

Jakob + MacFarlane

A New World Peace Center

Fraught with all of the contradictions that we found with this project, we wanted to somehow express our grief over what had happened at this site. Rather than proposing a New World Trade Center to replace what had fallen, we considered a design that would address the most pressing issues of the present. To talk of trade on this site seemed absurd. We felt a responsibility to propose a project that would pay respect to the lives lost and inspire attention to issues of global importance. We asked ourselves what could help rekindle hope and belief worldwide?

It was decided that the site should now, in some way, belong to the world and become a symbol of peaceful aspirations. We proposed a series of long, thin towers that resembled fingers. The spirit of the design was light and sensual. These inhabited fingers would light up and convey messages about issues of global concern, carrying information to the masses in a spirit of healing, sharing, and cooperation. The most appropriate statement seemed to be a structure that addressed the tragedy by paying close attention to the times in which we live.

THE WORLD BRIDGE
VIEW FROM JERSEY CITY

W O R L D   B R I D G E

© EYTAN KAUFMAN NY, NY 2001

Born in Israel in 1934, Eytan Kaufman received his bachelor of architecture from the Technion Israel Institute of Technology in 1960. He worked in Africa, England, and Israel before coming to the United States in 1966, where he studied with Buckminster Fuller and received a master of science from Southern Illinois University in 1970. He came to New York in the same year. In 1975 he founded his own firm, Eytan Kaufman Design and Development, which specializes in developing residential and commercial space.

Eytan Kaufman Design and Development

The World Forum and the World Bridge

This proposal has two separate entities. The first is the World Forum, occupying the sixteen-acre former site of the World Trade Center. It is dedicated to the time prior to September 11, 2001, with a permanent memorial recording and commemorating the loss of victims who perished during the destruction of the Twin Towers. The Forum is intended to be international in its focus, serving people of all nations. Its focal point is a dome that features continuously updated global information projected on its interior surface. Other components, such as cultural facilities and office space, will be contained in the buildings surrounding the plaza. The buildings will not exceed twelve stories in height.

In response to the magnitude of this tragedy a bridge connecting the World Trade Center site and the financial district of Jersey City is proposed as a second entity. The bridge is a metaphor for reaching out to the world and to the future. The World Bridge should become

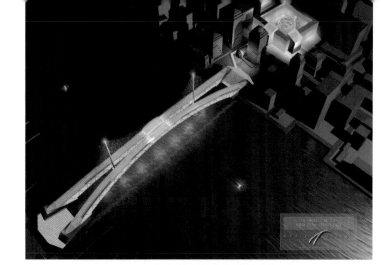

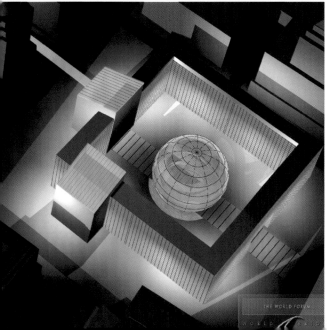

the highest engineering challenge. It is people-oriented and its proposed location over the Hudson River is unique and most exciting. The bridge is nonvehicular. It has its own internal transportation for goods and people, utilizing automated cars and travelators. The top of the bridge is a multilevel pedestrian promenade, reached by means of steps and escalators. It is used as a green park with many amenities. Below the green promenade there is a shopping street. The other floors would contain office space, hotel accommodation, theaters, galleries, and restaurants. The bridge would become an entire neighborhood, not comparable to any other.

Because of its unique character the bridge would attract a great deal of tourism, which will considerably enhance the economy of lower Manhattan as well as boost the economy of Jersey City. The bridge is approximately one mile long. It is 250 feet above water at the peak, providing sufficient clearance for maritime navigation. The distance between its piers is two thousand feet. The bridge contains about six million square feet of usable space. It is hoped that such a large and daring project will be a positive and inspiring contribution to the redevelopment of lower Manhattan. It would become a world landmark and provide a spiritual heritage for future generations.

Sheila Kennedy and her partner Frano Violich are cofounders of Kennedy & Violich Architecture. KVA explores ways to integrate architecture and infrastructure as a response to emerging programs and problems in contemporary culture. The work of Kennedy & Violich has been exhibited at the San Francisco Museum of Modern Art, the Museum of Modern Art in New York, and the Cooper-Hewitt National Design Museum.

Kennedy & Violich

Water and Land, Local Life and Gloabal Reach

Is it possible to imagine a memorial that is not excluded from everyday life; a memorial that engages the architectural scale of a building envelope and remembers by inscribing itself into the shared public infrastructure of the city? The vivid collective memory of the attacks forever alters the perception of the skyscraper and puts the absoluteness of its boundaries into question. The magnitude of lives lost and lives changed by these events establishes the possibility of a new relationship between the scale of the memorial and the architectural facade of a tall building. The memorial is projected as an active facade of individual panels, one for each victim. The panels are woven into a flexible, reflective cladding surface that serves as a communications network, engaging the luminous qualities of light on the New York waterfront. The configuration of this architectural cladding creates passages between water and land, between local life and global reach, between the city's public transportation infrastructure at ground level and its aerial telecommunications at the urban skyline.

The massing strategy is based on a respect for the uncontestable authenticity of the two World Trade tower sites. The footprints of both sites remain visible as voids in a fabric of smaller towers. This introduces an intermediate collective urban scale that supports a resilient and dense public urbanism never realized in the design of the World Trade Center. A new waterway, the length of the World Trade Center, is introduced from the Hudson River to allow an approach by water to the memorial at the southwest tower. The freestanding volume of this tower is defined

VIEW OF MEMORIAL CLADDING AND PUBLIC LOBBY

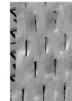

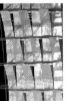

CLADDING STUDIES

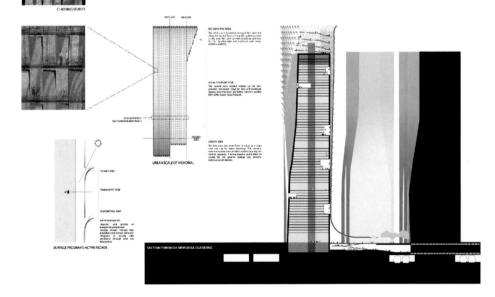

URBAN SCALE OF MEMORIAL

SURFACE PROGRAMS: ACTIVE FACADE

SECTION THROUGH MEMORIAL CLADDING

by the joining of the memorial surfaces rising from either side of the foundations of the World Trade towers. The memorial cladding and the interior volume create a vertical public gathering space moving up through the building, which could be one of four Nobel Peace Centers currently being planned for different sites across the world.

The urban proposal recovers the waterfront for public use and creates a new port for lower Manhattan, a public transportation hub that integrates the city's commuter ferry with MTA and PATH trains. The World Trade Center foundations are horizontal and vertical thresholds for the daily passages of people to and from the subway and waterfront. The memorial cladding is imagined as a porous, delicate surface array of emissive composites made up of many sending and receiving devices. Images and signals transmitted or received from New York pass through the array of the memorial cladding, making it a communications threshold that is both global and local in its performance.

The certainty of the World Trade Center site stands in contrast to what remains unknown. The realities of the interconnected world are still unfolding. These conditions of porosity extend from economic, national, and urban boundaries to the cladding materials of architecture. Flexible at its curved upper edges, the memorial surface plays with the light. As it changes color and moves with the wind, it is never in the same place. The memorial presents by its physical scale the magnitude of what is lost, and collaborates with the public's imagination by refusing to produce a singular or final understanding of these events.

VIEW FROM PARK ROW   VIEW FROM TRIBECA ROOFTOP

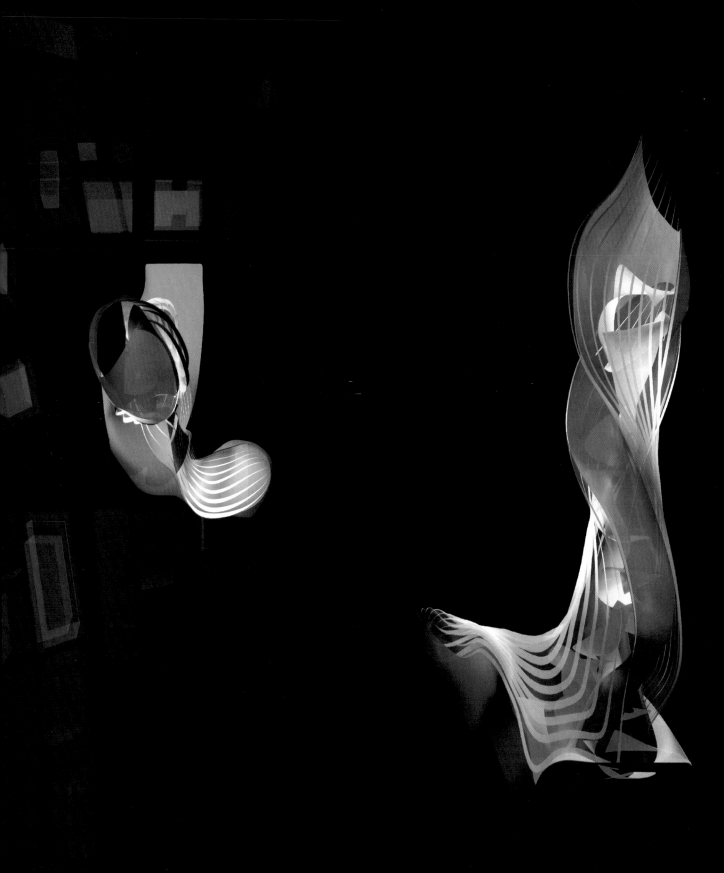

Tom Kovac has taught, lectured, and exhibited throughout Europe, Japan, and the United States. Current projects by his office, Tom Kovac Architecture, range from experimental conceptions and digital environments to urban planning projects. Kovac is currently working on the Digital Design gallery in Melbourne, creating Art Capsule to be exhibited in the NSA Exhibition at the Pompidou Centre in Paris, and collaborating with Alessi Italy for a new product range. He has recently been appointed by RMIT University as creative design director of *Curvedigital,* a joint project with the Melbourne Museum

Tom Kovac

Newly Emerging Configurations

Using software in unprecedented ways, we interrogated the organizational relationships within the complex, mapping the connections and representing them in space as an efficiency web. The traffic of people between these "attractors" was known, and we represented this in tubules with a thickness to scale. The volumes of space used in the old towers were then located as spheres. All this data was maximized for efficiency in space, the software pushing and pulling everything until it was in the optimum relationship to everything else. An envelope for this calculation was derived from a median topological mapping of the upper surface of the entire island. And the footprint of the site was held integral. We then programmed a surface into the interstices between the data, using the rule that the surface be trapped in the cage of the data, but never touch it. This formed the chassis for the design. The forms evoked those of Kiesler's Endless House. Into this we inserted a spiraling plane, governed by a rule that allowed for a travelator to climb endlessly in a braided stream across inclines that have the potential for future habitation.

Shared edges between the chassis and the spiral are enshrouded in glass, though the obvious form is not, so that in this design there is a contemplation of what was rather than a re-creation. Past dynamics are represented, but the design poses a question about the future: what spatial configurations correspond to the spatial schemata that are now emerging in us? Whereas in the past we were like Walter Mitty, daydreaming on the transit system in the anonymity of mass movement, now we are names in space, and we meet not anonymously, but intensely and face-to-face, when we must and where we must, on the oblique, much as slopes in Switzerland are occupied.

Krueck & Sexton, a Chicago-based architecture firm, is recognized for its innovative and sophisticated approach to design as well as the impeccable execution of its buildings. The practice is founded on the idea that a well-designed building should surpass the expectations of both client and architect. The firm achieves this through a hands-on engagement with every aspect of a design problem, by challenging assumptions and rethinking conventional methods.

Krueck & Sexton

Reflection of America's Dynamic Strength

This proposal is an affirmation of life, of the vitality of the city, and of our country's most fundamental values. Glass occuli memorializing the dead are located on the footprints of the original towers. Suspended at the plaza level, they are inscribed with the names of the dead and continuously washed by a thin layer of water. A fragment of the original facade marks the corner of where the North Tower once stood. The exterior of the building is a changing and ever-flexible skin, reflecting the freedoms and the dynamic strength of America. The transparent and light-weight structure placed along Church Street is lifted into the air, welcoming people to this sacred ground.

Daniel Libeskind is an international figure in architectural practice and urban design. Born in Poland in 1946, Libeskind became an American citizen in 1965. He studied music in Israel (on an America-Israel Cultural Foundation scholarship) and in New York. He left music to study architecture, receiving his professional architectural degree at New York City's Cooper Union for the Advancement of Science and Art in 1970 and a postgraduate degree in history and theory of architecture at the School of Comparative Studies at Essex University in 1972. In 1989 Daniel Libeskind won the competition for the Jewish Museum Berlin, which opened to the public in January 1999.

Daniel Libeskind

Stone and Spirit

Following the attacks that destroyed the World Trade Center, one has to evaluate architecture on completely new terms. It is a delicate task to ask what should be built in place of such an icon, especially given the power of its destruction. The significance of the site of the World Trade Center has changed dramatically. This is no longer a fully commercial site because of the number of innocent people murdered there. Be it a skyscraper, a low-rise complex, or a park developed on the site, the real question is about memory, and the future of that memory is what remains paramount. Beyond the obvious possibility of maintaining the ruins as a memorial or by creating a "memorial space," the urban strategy would have to incorporate a new understanding of form and function, one which has been altered by the irreversibility of what has happened. It must be a response that takes into consideration the relationships between the uniqueness of a site and its global significance; fragility and stability; stone and spirit. Whatever is built will have to acknowledge the permanent loss. This emptiness will remain and cannot be obliterated by any building. The trauma created by this event compels and challenges one to address a new process through which architecture responds.

LOT-EK is an architecture studio based in New York City, founded in 1993 by Ada Tolla and Giuseppe Lignano. Since then, LOT-EK has been involved in residential and commercial projects both in the U.S. and abroad, as well as exhibition design and site-specific installations for major cultural institutions and museums. Besides heading their professional practice, Tolla and Lignano currently teach at Parsons School of Design's Graduate School of Architecture, in New York. They also lecture in major universities and cultural institutions throughout the U.S. and abroad, including Columbia University, Yale University, E.T.H. Zurich, and Bartlett and Royal College of Art, London.

LOT-EK

Reconnecting Downtown

Our proposal for the World Trade Center site in lower Manhattan is based on the absence generated on September 11, wherein rebuilding and memorializing become one in the process of rethinking and reconnecting downtown. There is a value to a depression in a dense urban condition. In the hyper-density of lower Manhattan, the void left by the towers is more than a symbol of violence. It also reveals elements of the city that generally go unseen. The void is the "bathtub" dug during the construction of the towers, a pit seven stories deep and the size of four city blocks. The bathtub accentuates and depresses the void, creating an edge, a fracture that severs the site in both plan and section. The remains of the World Trade Center are treated as a contemporary archaeological site that values its memory while making a positive intervention, occupying the void and preserving its sanctity. Its history is something to live with, not something to obscure. The ground becomes something to look at, but not to walk upon, while the bathtub remains a space of activity. Existing subways and PATH trains together with the webs of infrastructure (water, cable, sewage, and electricity lines) occupy the void. This is not an archaeology of disaster, but an archaeology of the city.

We propose to reconnect the streets interrupted by the previous towers' construction. East–west streets are extended through the bathtub as pedestrian bridges reaching the World Financial Center and Battery Park City. Consisting of two parallel sets of modified containers, these public pathways are suspended in the bathtub by a light framework. Compressed in the space between the rows of

containers, a series of translucent cells adds new public functions along these pedestrian paths. These paths are about journey and interaction as much as they are about destination. Along the edge of the tub, eight towers are generated, extruding the space defined by the void and the existing streets. These extrusions are severed by the edge of the bathtub, exposing their inner concrete construction. The facade overlooking the tub is contaminated by a fragmented arrangement of horizontal translucent volumes, elevators, and containers. Elevators intersect with the pedestrian bridges below, folding horizontal circulation into vertical transportation. Fragmented channels, acting like city streets, meet with elevators and provide horizontal circulation along the facade. A set of tunnels, made of shipping containers, penetrates the building and projects out into the void, serving dual roles, reaching the different functions located in the buildings and entering the void as contemplative spaces.

As the future of lower Manhattan is at the core of an ongoing debate, the height of the towers is not predetermined. Each tower can grow up to over one hundred floors over time. The vertical growth is connected to, and becomes an indicator of, new uses for lower Manhattan, reflecting financial expansion as well as public psychological comfort.

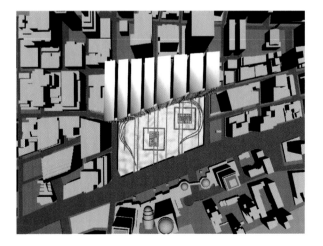

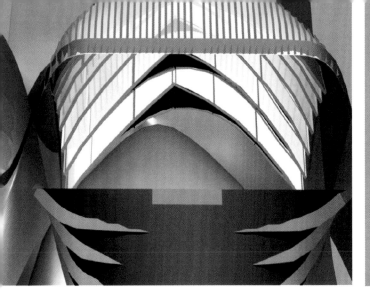
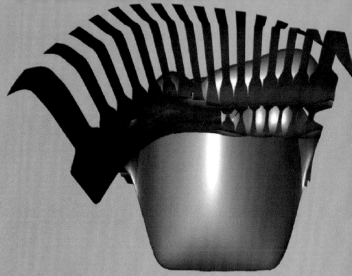

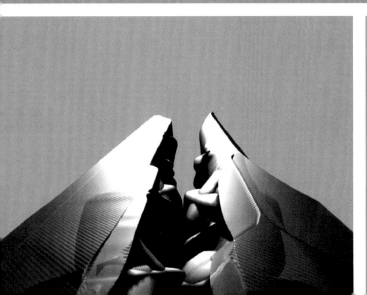
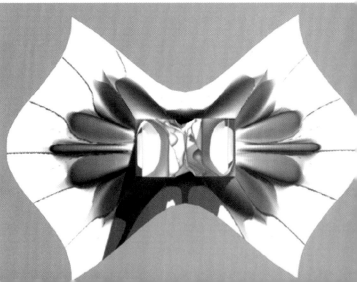

Greg Lynn FORM is leading architecture and design projects that vary in scale from a kilometer-long building to a teapot. Scheduled for completion in 2005 is a radical transformation of a 500-unit, eleven-story housing block in the Bijlmermeer outside of Amsterdam that completely reorganizes the housing block into aerial neighborhoods. Greg Lynn FORM also has two interior-design projects that use a heat-and-vacuum-formed PET plastic wall system. Greg Lynn teaches at the University of California at Los Angeles and was just named master professor at the University for Applied Arts in Vienna.

Greg Lynn FORM

Defensive Design and Technology

The attack on the World Trade Center marks the lack of distinction between military and urban space. The use of commercial aircraft as weapons and the targeting of office towers both represent the collapse of boundaries between global military conflict and everyday life. There is no return once these distinctions disappear. From now on, new skyscrapers, whose size, location, and design make them significant targets of terrorism, will need to incorporate defensive military design and technology. This return to medieval and Renaissance architectural and urban design—when defensibility and resistance to siege were primary design factors which forced architects to study trajectories of projectiles, maneuverability of troops, and resistance of materials—will significantly impact the design of buildings and cities today.

The transfer of military thinking into daily life is inevitable and any true security is futile. The memorial to the victims of terrorism at the World Trade Center as well as the redevelopment of the site must acknowledge this collapse between everyday life and international conflict, between global commerce and warfare, and between civic monuments and military targets. Before the design of the memorial and the rebuilding of the site, a statement of ambitions for the future of the site must be made.

Iñigo Manglano-Ovalle is an artist who uses photography, video, sound, and sculpture to create works that illuminate our notions of personal identity and community. Manipulating the conceptual, the sensory, and the scientific, his art extends from the molecular construct of DNA to the larger-than-life perspective of modern architecture. In the process, he creates compelling installations that stand out for their intelligence, elegance, and artistry. In 2001 he was named a John D. and Catherine T. MacArthur Foundation Fellow.

Iñigo Manglano-Ovalle

41° North, 74° West

This sound sculpture originated as an audio recording of wind noise, at which time the windspeed was twelve miles per hour, in the direction of 300° northwest. It was recorded at 41° north latitude and 74° west longitude in lower Manhattan, at an elevation of 1350 feet, on April 28, 2001.

This recording was made as part of an ongoing activity of collecting ambient sounds in urban sites. The original recording was archived for possible use in sound and/or video projects. In November 2001, this material was selected and edited into an infinite loop to be played back on twin parabolic speakers suspended above the listener. During the project's installation no information other than the title, *41°N, 74°W,* is provided that may refer to the events of September 11, 2001.

Nathan McRae was born in 1973 in Burlington, Vermont. He studied art, architecture, and business, earning a professional degree in architecture from the University of Oregon, and also studied architecture in Rome and Copenhagen. From 1996 to 1998 he worked at BML Architects in Portland, Oregon. Since 1998 he has practiced architecture in New York with Keenen/Riley, working on projects ranging from new large office and residential buildings to interior renovations.

Nathan McRae

Preservation of Loss

This building preserves the voids where the World Trade Center towers once stood by maintaining them as negative space within the new skin. The memorial is the preservation of the loss. The transparent exterior skin and its proximity to the interior voids allow a ghosted reading of the profiles of the original World Trade Center towers, which appear and disappear depending on the perspective of the observer. The voids provide transparency and penetration of light to the interior. At night, they are lit from within. The voids are accessible to the public at ground level, utilizing the footprints of the towers and their empty volumes as space for reflection.

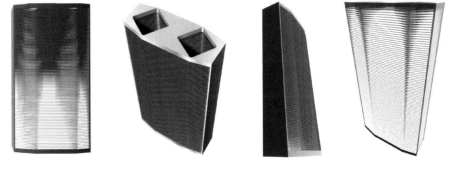

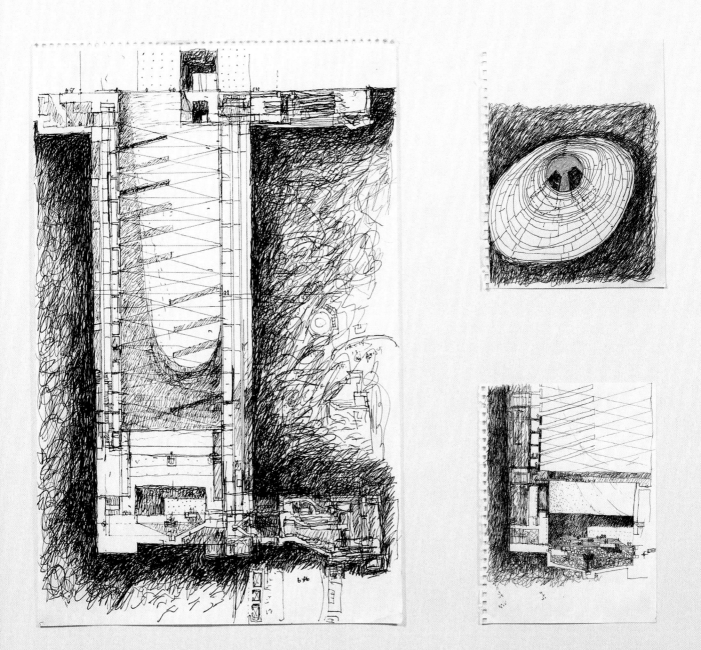

Samuel Mockbee (1944–2001) was an architect, artist, and alumni professor at Auburn University's School of Architecture, where he was cofounder and director of the Rural Studio. Mockbee and students from the university designed and built houses for impoverished families and communities in Hale County, Alabama. In the words of critic Robert Campbell, Mockbee proved "that architecture can still be a fine art and a social service at the same time." His legacy lives on at the Rural Studio, which continues to initiate new projects.

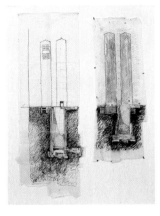

Samuel Mockbee

Skyward-Looking Subterranean Cultural Center

Samuel Mockbee conceived of this project from the hospital in the final hours of his life in late December. He described it over the phone as dark in nature, but, like Mockbee himself, it is in fact uplifting. Two towers rise higher than the originals, but the centerpiece of the design is a pit dug 911 feet into the ground with a memorial reflection pool and place for worship at the bottom. The underground complex is accessible by elevators and by a spiraling walkway that would allow visitors to gaze back up at the towers and the sky above. A subterranean cultural center and memorial chapel, located to the right of the pit in the drawings, are also part of the design.

As someone who respected every individual he met and considered civic and personal responsibility an integral part of his work as an architect, Samuel Mockbee would have been an ideal participant in the effort to rebuild and replan the World Trade Center.

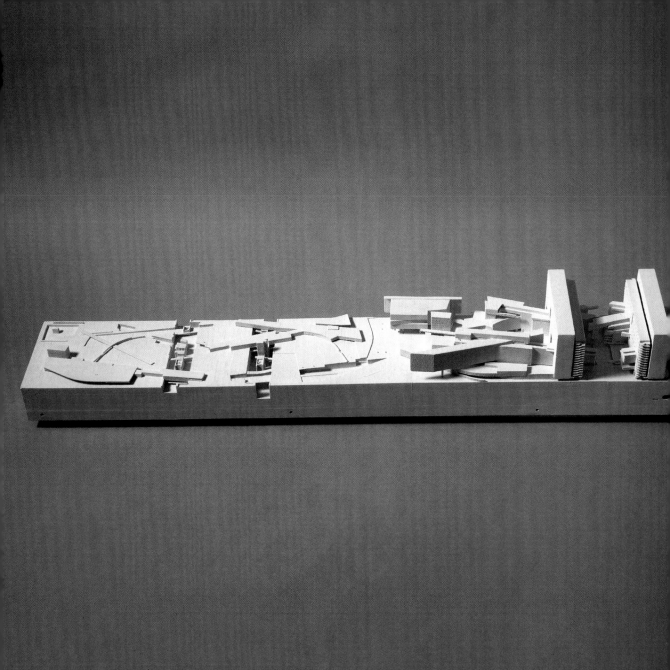

Morphosis was founded in 1972 to develop an architecture that would eschew the normal bounds of traditional forms and materials and surpass the limiting dualism of modern and postmodern. The firm is currently comprised of forty architects and designers directed by Thom Mayne. A significant percentage of the firm's work has been commissioned through international design competitions, including the University of Toronto Graduate Student Housing in Canada and the Diamond Ranch High School in California. They are currently in the design-development and construction-document phases for several significant public-sector projects, including a federal courthouse in Eugene, Oregon, the federal building in San Francisco, and the NOAA Satellite Control Center in Washington, D.C.

Morphosis

Balancing the World

Out of the twin ruins will emerge generative matter, evidence of the recent past, instigating new potentialities—a total transformation, a place where human experience and aesthetic sensibilities are interwoven in total freedom, demonstrating an interest in the balance and intertextuality of our world and all of its facets, political, economic, cultural, and ecological.

Eric Owen Moss received a bachelor of arts degree from the University of California at Los Angeles in 1965, and master of architecture degrees from both the University of California at Berkeley's College of Environmental Design in 1968 and from Harvard University Graduate School of Design in 1972. Eric Owen Moss Architects, located in Culver City, California, has been designing and building award-winning architecture since 1973. Current projects include the Mariinsky Cultural Center in St. Petersburg and the new Queens Museum of Art in New York. The firm's latest completed buildings are The Stealth, an office for a postproduction film firm; The Beehive, offices and a conference facility for medschool.com; and The Pterodactyl, an office building on top of a parking structure.

Eric Owen Moss

Two Pairs of Shadows

A park,
A stone park.
Hollow the site,
Down to the river wall,
Down to the trains,
Deep down.

Two pairs of shadows,
Shadows standing still.
Shadow 1: the first hit.
Shadow 2: the second hit.
Shadow 3: the first collapse.
Shadow 4: the second collapse.

The first pair:
           The way in and the way down and
           the way up and the way out
The second pair:
           Seats . . . only in shadow.

Ben Nicholson is British born, and was educated at the Architectural Association, Cooper Union, and Cranbrook Academy. He currently teaches architecture at the Illinois Institute of Technology in Chicago, where he has lived for the past fourteen years. As part of a long-standing interest in American culture, he recently contributed to Hartmut Bitomsky's documentary film *B-52* (2001). He has exhibited at several institutions and was named a fellow of the Chicago Institute for Architecture and Urbanism. His current projects include *The Hidden Geometric Pavement in Michelangelo's Laurentian Library,* a book that muses over numbers, geometry, and the structure of knowledge (2004).

Ben Nicholson

The World: Who Gets It and Who Wants It?

Perhaps what was remarkable about the World Trade Center is that its given name purported to suggest that the edifice was the center of world trade. When the towers were removed they took along with them a myriad of links and responsibilities that course throughout the globe, touching every aspect of life. The proposed project takes the stance that it is less important to adjust the shape and size of a new World Trade Center and more important to restructure the infrastructure of the whole world. To this end a satire entitled *The World: Who Gets It and Who Wants It?* has been composed to describe a vision of a world order in which a new World Trade Center could relax its guard against further assault. The one hundred billion dollars that the United States has pledged to address the world's wrongs is conceptualized as a large seed grant with which to build this new vision. The task at hand is to lessen the fury of the third world's railing against America's apparent waste, misuse of resources, vice, and purposelessness.

The first part of the text describes the Bilateral Peace Corps, a federally funded international program which searches out American values, and then discovers them in the form of former recipients of the 1960s Peace Corps programs. The Bilateral Peace Corps sets up cells in the meeting places of twelve-step programs and then fans out across the country, teaching Americans how to live and appreciate simple pleasures in a distended hyper-technological culture.

The second section outlines a complete restructure of the U.S. federal government, making provision for new agencies such as Birth & Control, the Credit

Card Cemetery, the Food & Packaging Administration, and a host of other activities that regulate and promote the new society. "Urbs Americana," reproduced here, is included in this section.

The final part of the text deals with international policy and largely focuses on the rebuilding of Jerusalem under American care, it being the seeming responsibility of every world power throughout history to take custody of the unruly city. The building program, a capitalist architectural jihad, accommodates all the hopes and aspirations of the three Abrahamic faiths in a harmonious display of architectural wherewithal. America extends its constitutional mandate for religious freedom to this epicenter of world theo-politics.

Urbs Americana: New York City

New York City, naturally adverse to any sort of handout from the federal government, will build and pay for an entirely new building type to replace the World Trade towers. In an act of supreme generosity, New York gives Newark, New Jersey, the federal money to build a new financial center for the world. New York passes the mantle of being the fiscal center of the free world on to its natural sparring partner, in preference for a higher calling that is in keeping with New York's intrinsic, unpredictable sense of self-preservation and dignity.

Outside of the appalling death and destruction of the urban apocalypse, the haunting specter we are left with is that the disaster created a micro–weather system of bureaucracy and swirling winds of Sheetrock dust intermingled with flakes of paper, bearing inconsequential meanings from the sky. Against this backdrop, what then goes in the hole to replace this architectural holocaust, for who in their right mind would step into an elevator of another 110-story building? New York must cede the mighty greenback to Newark, on condition that any new towers are designed according to the plans of Saul Steinberg.

New York is now readied to move on to greater acts of statehood, philanthropic majesty, and raw power. The first hint of the change is that the World Trade Center blocks are rezoned: a radical change of use is decreed, from it being a space dedicated to business to a space for the exercise of the quid pro quo. Similar to the Monument to Wealth built beneath the Washington Mall, a hole is prepared at Ground Zero on the site of the former World Trade Center. This time, a shaft five hundred feet deep and the same width as the diameter of the dome of Jerusalem's Dome of the Rock is cut into the granite beneath New York City. At its bottom a mold is prepared whose inner surface area exactly equals the volume of gold currently held in the United States. Once the liquid gold has been poured, the granite mold is chipped apart and a simple earth surface is prepared around the luminous ball for people to walk upon.

At ground level, a series of seven labyrinths are laid out on the sixteen-acre site, each a meditation on the nature of the path between the outside and the inside, between the self and the goal. Around the rim of the hole in which resides the Fed's bullion ball, a stone parapet is built for visitors to stare down at the marvel of accumulated wealth glowing at the bottom of the hole. A double spiral staircase winds around the sidewall of the hole, permitting access to the sphere from the earth's surface. A shaft is sunk beside the hole, into which is inserted an elevator for the use of the infirm, which will be made available to those who present the necessary credentials. There is no need for any security whatsoever, as it is impossible to remove the bullion ball due to its staggering weight and unstable mobility.

Visitors are welcome to visit the bullion sphere on the condition that they are completely naked by the time they reach the base of the hole. Pilgrims of wealth discard their clothing while they walk, run, or stumble down the ramp, throwing clothing and accessories in heaps onto the pavement, thus removing the desire for theft or the will to scratch initials on the ball with a solitaire diamond. The naked humans spread-eagle themselves against this icon of materialism, some frantically baring their teeth in a desperate attempt to have some of the national wealth or at least be able to leave their mark upon it. Once satiated by the mesmerizing power of the bullion ball, the naked forms stagger or dreamily glide up the ramp, rambling over clots of expensive bracelets intertwined with cheap acrylic sweatshirts. Blinded by gold, the folly of ownership, uncaring to determine which inner and outer clothing they owned, and unconscious of the glittering accessories they once lavished so much of their income on, the visitors emerge at the rim of the hole in a daze, where they are gently taken to one side and covered by a simple garment for the sake of public decorum.

The view from above, of telescopically diminutive figures crowding around the glowing element, is a simple yet unforgettable sight, perhaps overtaking the popularity of the Metropolitan Museum. Humanity is at last seen for what it is, a blob of reptilian creatures swarming and crawling over matter that they desperately desire to possess.

Away from this spectacle of consumerism, uptown on Forty-second Street, the United Nations building closes its mission for good. The whole operation is moved to its new location on a manmade island in the newly restored Dead Sea near Jerusalem. The billionaire mayor of New York announces that he will build a place for all the NGO's in the world, a counterpoint to organized government, called the UNGO. Every representative of any and every cause is invited to Manhattan to state his case and a new era of understanding is born. New York reestablishes its enfant terrible reputation, but this time that quality is safely institutionalized in UNGO, an organization created to go against the grain and make the voice of the little guy audible from a distance. New York is the center of it all, as she takes on the persona of enveloping political correctness at the international level.

Lastly, the precariously leaning wall of the old World Trade Center is welded back together and set up exactly where it was, after the manner of the dome left standing at Ground Zero where the Americans detonated a nuclear device in the midst of Hiroshima, that other marker of inhuman atrocity against an unknowing civilian population. The WTC monument would simply show how technology can be turned against itself, duplicating the central tenet of aikido, in which the power generated by the one is channeled by the other to go against itself. This monument serves to show the world the sting of technology's tail, the dangerous construct of hubris, in which the works of humankind can get horribly out of control, challenging their own seemingly inviolable circle in a scenario that only the Greek polytheistic writers acknowledged the dangers of and had the skill to express.

New York now fills out its boots, a senior city that has grown to a new stature, no longer alive to its own youth but joyful in maturity and content in its recurring memories. New York joins the ranks of the once-glorious cities of London, Shanghai, Rome, Kabul, Florence, and Moscow. Just as we now go to Florence to see the marvels of the Renaissance, we now visit New York to see the marvels of capitalism, a place where everything from culture to nourishment was bought for hard cash, and which attracted colonies of artists who produced things and thoughts to reflect this quirky opulence. In the same way that art historians flock to Florence to create beautiful, studied drawings in the manner of the masters, coached by tweedy professors with British accents, students of art will come to New York to bathe in the culture of its golden years. In the summer months, effete students of art will erratically flick paint at oversized canvases while an adoring daddy stands by, happy to have been able to give his darling daughter the culture that he wants and she has learned to crave.

Quaranic Quotable, on Sin City:

> When we resolve to raise a city, we first give warning to those of its people who live in its comfort. If they persist in sin, judgment is irrevocably passed and we destroy it utterly.
>
> —SURA 17:15

Lars Spuybroek is principal of NOX, an architecture office in Rotterdam. Since the early nineties he has been involved in the researching the relationship between architecture and media, often more specifically between architecture and computing. He was editor-publisher of two of the first magazines in a book format (*NOX* and *Forum*), made videos, and created interactive electronic artworks. During the last five years he has focused more specifically on architecture. His work has been exhibited all over the world, including a presentation at the Venice Biennale, 2000.

NOX

Oblique World Trade Center

We should try to find new urban strategies to deal with the huge, with global forces working on local situations. We should find ways to work against the homogeneous which are more open to the changes and unpredictability of life. Undeniably the skyscraper is the most successful building type of the twentieth century. However, we feel its generic reductionism, its passive stacking of human behavior, its manic monoprogramming will and should become obsolete and as a type it will have to be rethought, making a new evolutionary step of the megabuilding possible.

In rethinking the mega, the huge, we should be more concerned with the structure of the huge than its size. For this we should move away from top-down techniques toward bottom-up techniques. For obliqueWTC we reused the old wool thread modeling technique invented by Frei Otto and his team at the Institute for Lightweight Structures in the 1970s. In our case we used one wool thread for each core of the destroyed or damaged buildings on the former World Trade Center site. As an inverted model the wool threads hang straight down under the sole influence of gravity forces. When dipped into water and taken out again all threads reorganize themselves into a complex network (with the cohesive lateral forces of the water now added to the gravitational system), comparable to bone structure. The structure is not formed anymore by a simple extrusion of a plan, but self-organizes into a networked megastructure where the whole is larger than the sum of its parts.

We thicken each of the wool threads into a lean tower that merges and splits up as it moves upward. This enables the structure to comply with the New York zoning law that only allows high buildings to occupy 25 percent of the total site surface area. In this case however, the 25 percent is always positioned somewhere else, making it both into one single megabuilding with many (structural) holes in it or many thin towers that cooperate into one large structure. The towers sometimes act as a bridge, sometimes as a counterstructure for one another, and sometimes free themselves to become a smaller subtower. Most of the loads are transported through the honeycomb steel structure of the surface, which is helped by an interior column grid, which follows the diagonals of the towers. Also, the elevators form a highly complex structure of diagonals where at some platforms five or six different cores come together to form larger public areas. It is this network of elevators which makes the building not just a new type of tower, but a new type of urbanism. The elevators become an urban extension to the subway system: a punctuation of the street by a technological system to intensify its public functioning.

Generally all urban interactions within a Manhattan block only happen on street level, while all buildings blindly tower away from that level into a noninteractive side-by-sidedness. Here we renetwork the street into the tower itself. We read the wool thread diagram both structurally and programmatically, where the structural "diagonals" become a reemerging of Virilio's oblique: lateral, horizontal street forces are multiplied with the vertical stacking model of the skyscraper, resulting in an oblique tower.

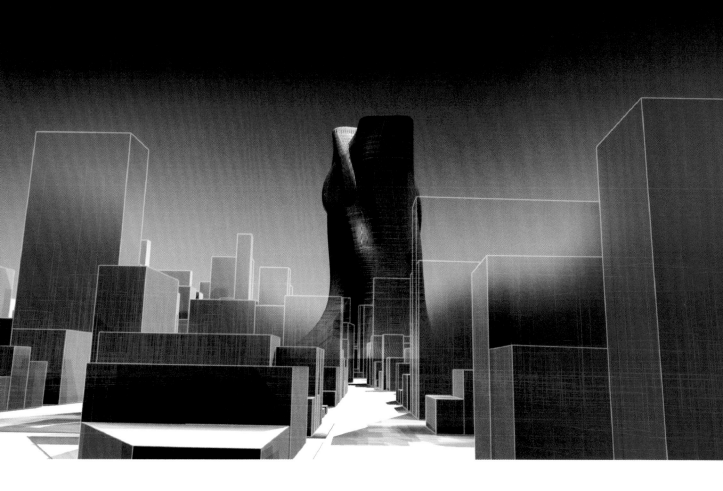

OCEAN north

OCEAN north, led by Tuuli and Kivi Sotamaa, Briger Sevaldson, and Michael Hensel, pursues practice-oriented and experimental design and research with the aim to investigate relations across scales, from small products to architecture and urban design. OCEAN north pursues an approach to urban design that acknowledges it as an interrelated design discipline that coordinates planned interventions with freely evolving changes of urban contexts.

A World Center for Human Concerns

Our collaborative study for a new World Center for Human Concerns proposes a space for all peoples and cultures, whether existing or emergent. The volume of the World Center for Human Concerns provokes a sensuous image of formation, continuity, and multiplicity. It remains intelligible whether one single object folds upon itself or divides, or whether two objects are entwined in conflict or fusion. The object is and becomes both one and many at the same time. As a memorial to the drama of September 11 and a statement against all acts of violence, the volume of the World Center inscribes within itself the volume of the previous Twin Towers, which are visible as vague figures through the textured and folded skin of the new building. Its spaces result from the draping and folding of the building skin, which articulate the building volume as a set of interstitial spaces that await their programmatic definition directly through shifting patterns of collective inhabitation. Through this approach the scheme seeks at this stage to be provocative toward emergent social and institutional arrangements, while pursuing a strategy of spatial differentiation through the material articulation of the building skin. Its surface geometry articulates spaces, while its material makeup and striated articulation (similar to that of the previous Twin Towers) enable a modulated transparency of both the skin and the spaces within and beyond it. This tension between formal ambiguity and articulation grants in every location a unique spatial experience for the beholder.

The scheme abandons the common high-rise organization of central service and circulation cores and uses instead the building skin as a space for circulation, with a large number of circulation channels nested within it. A second phase of the project focuses on the development of the basketlike circulation channel system into a structural principle, resulting in a system that will be less vulnerable to local disruption.

Instead of an impossible horizontal expansion of Manhattan and the obvious difficulties with vertical growth, the scheme proposes a thickening of the space of existing buildings by adding layers around them. With this approach arises a need for rethinking the question of daylight in deep plans and structures. By questioning an equal need for daylight, differentiated interior habitats can be articulated instead. Rain forests and oceans serve as an analogical model, where even in the lowest and darkest regions micro-ecologies flourish. This leads to a redefinition of what constitutes a twenty-four-hour city. So far this notion has implied available programs around the clock. An alternative could entail diverse daylight conditions at all times. The darker core might constitute a twenty-four-hour night program zone, while the outer and peripheral areas might enable a flexible negotiation of programs relative to changing light conditions.

For subsequent phases of the project, other design practices and experts will be invited to join the collaborative effort. It soon becomes evident that a scheme of this enormous scale needs to be treated like a section of city that emerges from the collective efforts of many actors. In this sense there can only be one conclusion: to be continued. . . .

Office dA

The work of Office dA is diverse in scope and scale, ranging from the broader scale of urban design and infrastructure to architecture, interiors, and furniture design. Most recently, in 2002, Office dA received a Design Award at the forty-ninth Progressive Architecture Awards for the Tongxian Art project. Tongxian Art is currently under construction in Beijing, China. Recent renovation projects include Mantra Restaurant in downtown Boston and the Harvard Graduate School of Design's architecture and urban design offices.

A New Skyscraper Paradigm

This proposal revolves around a new sacred ground: the footprints of the World Trade Center inscribed into the ground as a permanent index of the towers. Establishing the original site of the World Trade Center towers as a pair of public spaces, the proposal treats the remainder of the site as an opportunity to receive the city to a maximum capacity. On the site of the former Marriott Hotel and World Trade Center Plaza, we propose a new skyscraper. Polemically, innocently, or problematically, the proposal of a tall building is the core question. Will the skyscraper as a building type survive after September 11? And if not, can its abandonment secure any architecture from terror? We propose neither one nor two buildings, but a decidedly ambivalent structure oscillating somewhere in between. At its base, the tower emerges from the ground as two trunks growing from opposite corners of the site. As the building rises, the structures fuse into one, tapering at its top to incorporate the necessary communication antennae. Conceived neither as a classical type nor as a modern extrusion, the tower absorbs the benefits of both morphologies to evolve into a new paradigm.

The Skyscraper: Structure and Skin as Agents of Redundancy

In rethinking the skyscraper as a building type, we investigate three interpretations of structural models. The conventional steel frame (Seagram Building) achieves a considerable structural rigidity through the repetition of the grid and its lateral bracing—its corresponding curtain wall not contributing to its structural rigidity. The structural skin (World Trade Center) benefits from a reinforced outer membrane, while achieving maximum flexibility in its interior. A misreading of the Statue of Liberty suggests a compelling combination of the preceding models: a structural core and the potential for a structural skin as interpreted through the folded geometry of her copper robe. We propose a structural system that permeates both the skin and inner framework. Triangulated to join at every third floor, the system is able to achieve structural redundancy while leaving enough leasable space to remain sufficiently efficient. Diagonal bracing pierces floors in varied locations as the system navigates the variable geometry of the proposal; the mesh expands and contracts as it envelops different floor plates, programs, and sectional conditions.

Oosterhuis.nl is a multidisciplinary architectural firm, where architects, visual artists, Web designers, and programmers work together and join forces. The firm's portfolio encompasses a variety of projects in divergent fields of experience, including housing projects, exhibition pavilions, corporate business buildings, city planning tools, online experiences, interactive installations, and theoretical studies.

Oosterhuis.nl

Toward an E-motive Architecture

Everyone seemed at once horrified and fascinated by September 11. People were amazed to watch the impacts, over and over again. Only extremely disciplined individuals could resist watching. The questions I ask myself here are: How could architects in this extraordinary setting positively address people's fascinations by proposing a building? Should we and could we induce deep emotions by making architecture? My proposal for Ground Zero is to build a structure that lives in a permanent crisis; a structure that changes shape and content in real time; a structure that is comfortable with being in a process of permanent destruction and immediate healing of its wounds; a structure that is alive in real time.

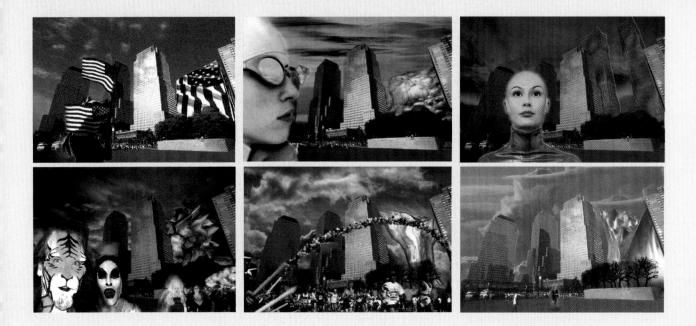

Imagine a constructive system that is put together as a three-dimensional grid of programmable cylinders. Forget everything you know about traditional buildings, about fixed columns and beams, about rigid facade panels. Imagine that every bit of the structure would be changeable, flexible in size and moldable in its curvature. Not only the walls could change, but also the floors, the ceilings, and the voids. Think of it as one continuum, like an everchanging swarm of building elements. Can it be done? Yes, and we know exactly how to do it. Does it cost a lot? Yes, the building will be twice as expensive, but it will perform at least three times more responsivly since it acts effectively according to external and internal forces, to the needs of its users. Would it benefit mankind? Yes. It would greatly enhance people's emotional attachment to the built environment. People would start to experience buildings and their immediate working and living environments as something highly natural, as something which is alive. They would love the unexpected changes in shape, they would be thrilled to just sit and watch the building move. And more than that, they would feel invited to take part in the action. Now we have found a way of getting rid of the rigidity of buildings. Now buildings can become interactive soft bodies, as a friend and playmate.

Imagine a large volume that can propagate itself upward reaching the height of the former Twin Towers, sideways to cover complete streets, and outward to the Hudson River to provide shelter on rainy days. Imagine the volume of this programmable building always taking different shapes, always prepared to react to events that happen in the city. Our proposal shows twelve different building configurations for the twelve months of the year 2012. The e-motive building architecture becomes a game people play. Am I naive to think this can be achieved? No, I am just taking a good look around me and I am willing to draw the logical conclusion of the invasion of distributed intelligence into our daily lives. Computational beauty may be the proper answer to destruction. E-motive architecture will embody beauty, local pride, and global awareness in real time.

Frei Otto

Berghalde 19 71229 Leonberg Tel. 0049-7152-41084
Fax.0049-7152-43908

To Mr. Max Protetch   Fax 212.691.4342
511 W 22ⁿᵈ Street, New York, N. Y. 10011-1109

Dear Max,
When you asked me to design a New World Trade Center I said, no I can't, because it is too early to make final decisions. But you convinced me to give at least my thoughts by sketching.

A new tower of Babel is not needed. But I think that there must remain a sign for memory. The site has to be cleared from all artefacts as steel, concrete etc. and to be protected as a world heritage in a peaceful city park with ponds and trees.
All human relicts will be collected within a hill, covered with earth from the victims' home countries, planted with flowers.
The remaining two big holes – full of water and surrounded by trees – are ponds of memory and prayer.
On a big world map, which is integrated in the pavement of an open space in the park, all countries at war are marked by lights, reminding of man's suffering. A special board announces continuously the number of all people killed by war from the 11 th September 2001 forward.

If a replacement of a World Trade Center is unavoidable for the near future I would see it as a low-raise green city on swimming platforms anchored in sight of Manhattan.

12 December 2001   Frei Otto

Frei Otto trained at the Technical University of Berlin from 1948 to 1952. In 1952 he established a studio at Zehlendorf and in 1957 he founded the Development Center for Lightweight Construction in Berlin. Seven years later he transferred the center's activities to the Institute for Lightweight Structures at the University of Stuttgart. Throughout his career, Otto has exhibited a gift for creating lightweight tentlike structures. He is well known for his design for the German Pavillion at the 1967 Montreal Expo and the 1972 Olympic Stadium in Munich. In 1972 New York's Museum of Modern Art organized a one-person exhibition *The Work of Frei Otto*. Otto has received many awards, including the 1974 Thomas Jefferson Medal and the 1998 Aga Khan Prize for Architecture.

Frei Otto

World Heritage in a City Park

Dear Max,

When you asked me to design a New World Trade Center, I said, no I can't, because it is too early to make final decisions. But you convinced me to give at least my thoughts by sketching.

A new tower of Babel is not needed. But I think that there must remain a sign for memory. The site has to be cleared of all artifacts of steel, concrete, etc., and to be protected as a world heritage in a peaceful city park with ponds and trees.

All human relics will be collected within a hill, covered with earth from the victims' home countries, planted with flowers.

The remaining two big holes—full of water and surrounded by trees—are ponds of memory and prayer.

On a big world map, which is integrated in the pavement of an open space in the park, all countries at war are marked by lights, reminding us of man's suffering. A special board announces continuously the number of all people killed by war from the 11th September 2001 forward.

If a replacement of a World Trade Center is unavoidable for the near future I would see it as a low-rise green city on swimming platforms anchored in sight of Manhattan.

Frei Otto
12 December 2001

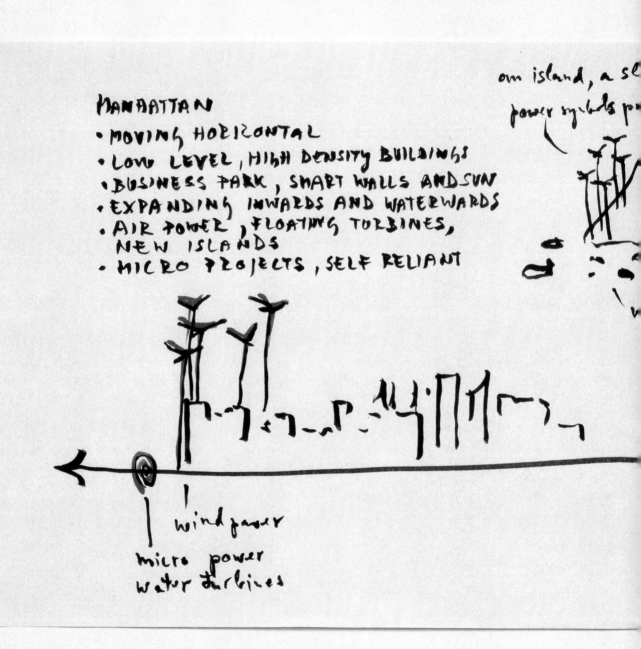

MANHATTAN
- MOVING HORIZONTAL
- LOW LEVEL, HIGH DENSITY BUILDINGS
- BUSINESS PARK, SMART WALLS AND SUN
- EXPANDING INWARDS AND WATERWARDS
- AIR POWER, FLOATING TURBINES, NEW ISLANDS
- MICRO PROJECTS, SELF RELIANT

own island, a se
power system po

wind power

micro power
water turbines

Marjetica Potrč is a Ljubljana, Slovenia, based artist and architect. Her work has been featured throughout Europe, the United States, and South America, including shows at the 1996 Sao Paulo Biennial, Skulptur Projekte 1997 in Muenster, the Guggenheim Museum, and Max Protetch Gallery. In addition, Potrč has received numerous awards, including grants from the Pollock-Krasner Foundation (1993 and 1999) and the Soros Center for Contemporary Arts, Ljubljana (1994), the Parque de la Memoria Sculpture Prize, Buenos Aires (2000), and the Hugo Boss Prize 2000, Guggenheim Museum.

Marjetica Potrč

Energy Unbound

My proposal is not about the form or function of some future structure on the site of the former Twin Towers. It is about energy. The idea is to make use of independent energy sources, such as wind, water, and solar power, as well as devices such as fuel cells, to generate power in Manhattan. I put emphasis on microenergy power. Take fuel cells: owners of fuel cells are not only able to produce enough energy for their households or businesses, but they can also upload the surplus energy to the existing power grid and thus share the energy with the city. In this way, individuals are empowered and the power supply is more evenly balanced. As for the construction itself, emphasis on energy and technology makes sense. Just think of smart walls. I have always thought of Manhattan as a generator of ideas. To make use of micro power on a large scale, such as a new complex on the World Trade Center site, would be a move in this direction. As for the visual impact, there is no doubt that windmills, micro water turbines, and solar energy would revitalize the New York skyline and seafront.

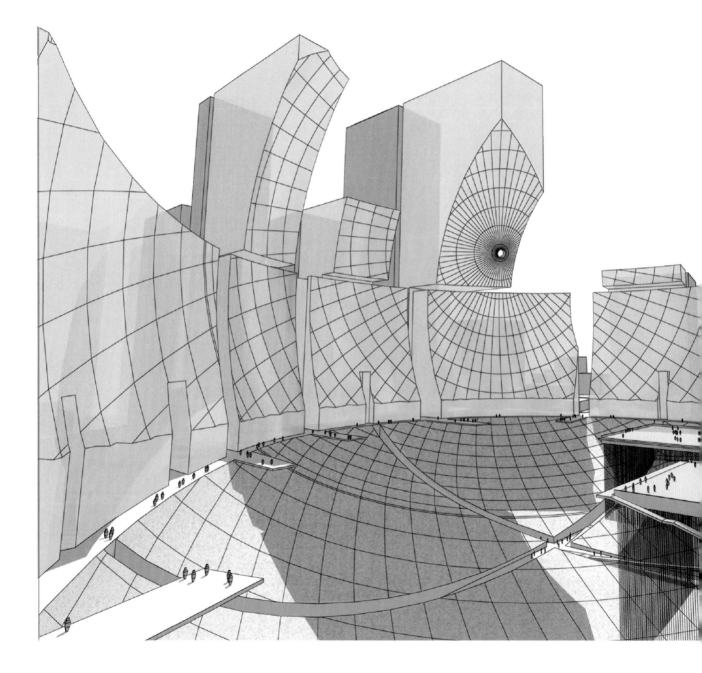

RoTo Architects was founded in 1991 by Michael Rotondi, FAIA, and partner Clark Stevens, AIA. RoTo has completed a wide range of project types of varying scope and complexity. In 1999 RoTo was selected to design the new La Jolla Playhouse and Play Development Center on the University of California at San Diego's campus and received an NEA grant with the Kohala Center in Hawaii for the creation of a new medical campus on the big island. In 2001 the firm won a national design competition for the LINC/Pitzer College Housing Complex in Ontario, California.

RoTo Architects

World Citizens Conference Center

Things change continuously at a frequency and rate that are generally comprehensible, intellectually and emotionally. Sometimes things change so radically in unexpected ways that there is no possibility of returning to our original position. This can be a positive thing. Tragedy brings us closer together at all scales of society. Our collective survival instinct is a great social equalizer, at least for a while. This time, however, things can be different. People are now talking to friends and strangers about how they feel and what they think. The full spectrum of emotions mixes with a broad range of intelligence to discuss and debate a most fundamental aspect of our existence: the line that separates humanity from inhumanity. This must continue indefinitely, and Ground Zero, New York City, should host the discussion.

The site of the World Trade Center has become the newest member of an exclusive set of places that are permanent records of a tragic human event of great magnitude. Our proposal is for a place of recollection, exchange, and renewal, either in solitude or in community. Our World Citizens Conference Center would be accessible to everyone for learning and teaching through formal and informal exchange formats, conflict resolution, a world conference of religion and wisdom traditions, world organizations working on humanitarian issues, and commercial service organizations that facilitate global humanitarian work. The new void of destruction within the city is vast; this vastness is in proportion to the historical transformation that is under way.

In our proposal, the site of the towers is marked with the green meadows of equal size to the building footprints. They are at city grade and are held up by thousands of columns memorializing those who were lost, so that people may walk among them. The World Trade Center will not be rebuilt but an equivalent amount of floor space and building mass will be reconstructed in the surrounding blocks. The new buildings will surround an enlarged Ground Zero site, shaped as a coherent elliptical volume, a kind of "Orphic Egg," which will be left open.

In contemplating the aerial photography of the damage and incomprehensible human loss, we became aware of the form of an upturned palm in the image of the now-blurred street grid and diagonals forming its lined topography. This form seemed an apt metaphor for the reconstruction, and perhaps healing, of the site:

> The palm of a hand is impassive.
> Fists and fingers have their agendas,
> but what rests in a palm is free to tell
> its silent truth.
> —DAVID JAMES DUNCAN

The shape of this restful palm, and the volume it held, appeared oval, reminiscent of the Orphic Egg, a symbol of transformation, rebirth, and creation. The vacant land sur-rounding the site—former parking lots, destroyed buildings, or open space—will be built upon. The streets coming from every direction will bring cars up to the back edge of these new buildings, but no further. The space of the streets will allow pedestrians to pass through the walk into or over the Ground Zero volume. The spatial orientation of this volume will align with an aperture in the surrounding new building mass, through which the sun will annually pass on September 11, at 8:46 A.M., Eastern Daylight Time. This illumination will be a permanent and inextinguishable memorial. The damaged buildings surrounding the site will be repaired with new "facades" of varying depth, which will provide additional building mass of up to eleven million square feet. This new building mass will form the "fingers" of the upturned palm that is the memorial zone. Within these perimeter buildings, the four elements of the World Citizens Conference Center will form a spatial and psychic buffer between the volume of remem-brance and the commerce of the city. A vertical threshold will separate the humanitar-ian activity within the inner layer from the protective commercial space that will line the outer layer of the new buildings. Our hope is that by linking these two modes of human activity, the deeper human exchange that is the only positive legacy of the tragedy may be perpetuated.

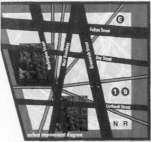

surface improvement diagram

As a tribute to human sacrifice on September 11, the two footprint areas of the former Trade Center towers are dedicated to commemoration of the firefighters - Fire Department of New York, and police officers - New York Police Department and Port Authority who lost their their lives in the disaster. It is proposed that these enclosures contain 440 evergreen trees. This program of planting will be extended throughout Manhattan neighborhoods - Bronx, Harlem, Brooklyn, Queens, Long Island and Staten Island - until there are enough trees in satellite areas to account for all of the near three thousand people killed by the terrorist attack. The memorial elements include:
· 440 American arborvitae trees - USA's dedicated "tree of site" - which grow to a height of seventy feet; plus near three thousand additional trees planted in other New York City neighborhood areas;
· Two water walls, adjacent to a below street level section of the South and West sides of Tree Memorial One, commemorating the names of the perished, while celebrating the value of water.

PREMISES:
The motivations behind this project are to:
· Celebrate people, not buildings
· Showcase human diversity, not homogenized commerce
· Encourage evolution and change, not rigid master planning

To accomplish the above, it is intended that the program will include:
· Strong representation of New York's ethnic and cultural diversity
· Dedication to ecologically responsible and structurally sustainable architecture
· Memorial areas dedicated to the fire and police officers

Greenwich and Barclay Streets looking South

West Broadway and Barclay Street looking South

West and Albany Streets looking North

West and Murray Stree

Maiden Lane looking West

Fulton Street looking West

SITE PROPOSAL:
The motivating vision behind the pla include existing streets, scale referen varieties of commerce, environmenta ethical design principles and safety s commensurate with an area of this si
· Integration of the site with the ne extending the East / West streets (Cortlandt) and the North / South st and Washington) - designation for
· Reconnection of the former subway improved total site areas pedestrian extensive underground retail space
· Mixed use buildings of variable he business offices, commercial retail, and residential uses, connected at pedestrian walkways and rooftop g
· Green plazas, parks, and areas for
· Washington and Greenwich "built- circulation connections and shelter
· Total site sustainable architecture a
· Canals utilizing the tidal changes a activate the flowing movement of t

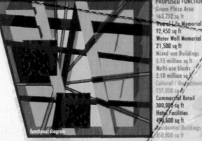

functional diagram

PROPOSED FUNCTIONS:
Green Plaza Area
163,750 sq ft
Tree of Life Memorial
92,450 sq ft
Water Wall Memorial
21,500 sq ft
Mixed-use Buildings
5.15 million sq ft
Multi-use blocks
2.10 million sq
Cultural / Recreational
255,000 sq ft
Commercial Retail
300,000 sq ft
Hotel Facilities
490,600 sq ft
Residential Buildings
650,000 sq ft

The purpose of this project is to re-build the World Trade Center site area with the following functional characteristics:
· Appropriate New York City urban scale and density
· Mixture of office, retail, cultural, entertainment and residential uses
· Assortment of green plazas and public spaces

longitudinal section bisecting at Tree Me

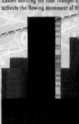

FORMER FUNCTIONS:
Office Space
11.0 million sq ft
Retail area
300,000 sq ft
Hotel Facilities
818 rooms

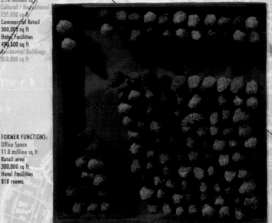

former site diagram

aerial site plan

NEW WORLD TRADE CENTER DESIGN PROPOSAL by S I T E - JAMES WINES - DENISE MC LEE - STOMU MIYAZAKI - PATRICK H

SITE is an internationally known, multidisciplinary environmental arts and architecture organization located in New York City. The studio offers a wide variety of design services—including buildings, public spaces, landscapes, interiors, graphics, and industrial products. SITE's capacity to work in so many fields is based on a philosophy that sees all of the arts as a fusion of related ideas. SITE was founded in 1970 by James Wines and presently includes a team of architects, artists, landscape designers, and technicians. The primary purpose of the organization is to communicate effectively with people through municipal projects that advocate social and environmental responsibility.

SITE

Memorial Gardens, Sustainable Urban Architecture

The SITE proposal for the New World Trade Center is based on a commemoration of the tragic events of September 11, a respect for the history of Wall Street architectural scale and density, the urban design wisdom of a more flexible alternative to replace the original WTC site plan, and the need to reestablish Lower Manhattan's natural characteristics of organic neighborhood development, commercial variety, and cultural diversity.

The features of the SITE project are:

- Resurrection of the former lower Manhattan street connections as the basis of a new site plan (distributed by construction of the original World Trade Center), including the east–west extensions of Fulton, Cortlandt, and Dey Streets and the north–south continuation of Greenwich and Washington Streets.

- Creation of an inherently flexible master plan for the site that invites evolution and change, allows for mixed-use commercial development (office, residential, hotel, retail, cultural), and encourages a strong representation of New York's ethnic diversity.

- Elimination of the inflexible concept of megaskyscrapers and vast open spaces in favor of a variety of closely spaced ten- to thirty-story buildings, designed by a variety of architects to provide the same amount of rental space as the lost World Trade Center towers.

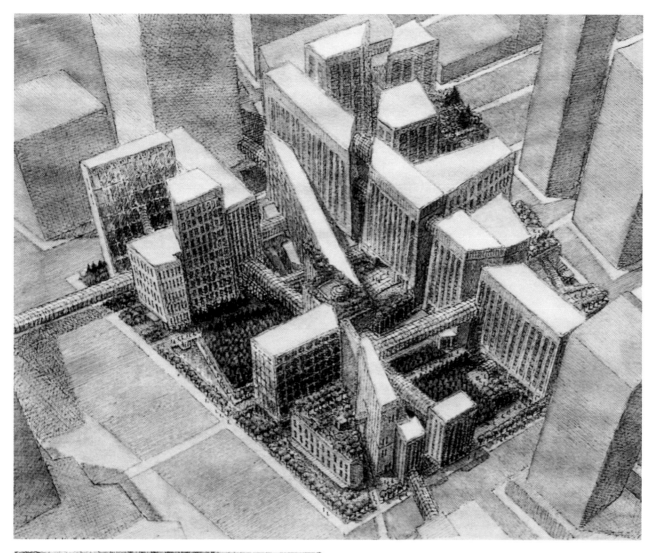

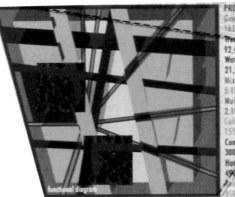

PROPOSED FUNCTIONS
Green Plaza Area
163,750 sq ft
Tree of Life Memorial
92,450 sq ft
Water Wall Memorial
21,500 sq ft
Mixed-use Buildings
5.15 million sq ft
Multi-use blocks
2.10 million sq ft
Cultural / Recreational
155,000 sq ft
Commercial Retail
300,000 sq ft
Hotel Facilities
490,600 sq ft
Residential Buildings
350,000 sq ft

• Placement of two memorial landscapes in the footprint areas where the World Trade Center towers once stood, for the planting of 440 American arborvitae trees, which grow to a height of seventy-five feet, to commemorate the police officers and firemen who lost their lives.

• Planting seven memorial tree lines that radiate outward from the center of the New World Trade Center site to Harlem, the Bronx, Queens, Long Island, Brooklyn, Staten Island, and New Jersey. These satellite memorials pay tribute to all of New York through the planting of one memorial tree for every civilian life lost.

• Creation of a below-street-level water wall structure and pool that honors the names of all of the World Trade Center victims, celebrates the value of water during the lifesaving and cleanup operations, and recognizes the natural phenomenon of the tides going in and out.

• Encouragement of sustainable architecture and resource-saving green design principles in all new construction for the site.

Note on the memorial gardens: In tribute to the human sacrifice on September 11, the two footprint areas of the original World Trade Center buildings are dedicated to commemorating the lost members of the New York Fire Department, the New York Police Department, and the Port Authority. It is proposed that these areas contain 440 evergreen trees as a celebration of growth and life over destruction and death. This planning program is intended for expansion throughout all of the New York neighborhoods—Bronx, Harlem, Brooklyn, Queens, Long Island, and Staten Island—until there are enough trees planted in satellite areas to account for all the nearly three thousand people killed in the terrorist attack.

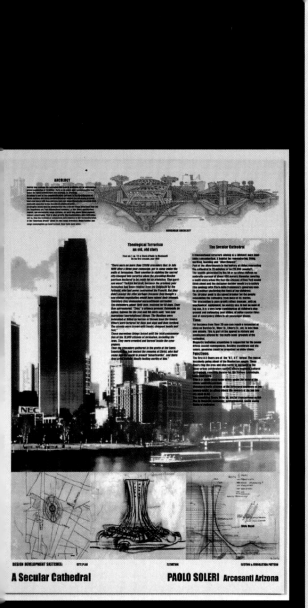

ARCOLOGY

NOREANOAH ARCOLOGY

Theological Terrorism
an old, old story

The Secular Cathedral

DESIGN DEVELOPMENT SKETCHES: SITE PLAN

A Secular Cathedral

PAOLO SOLERI Arcosanti Arizona

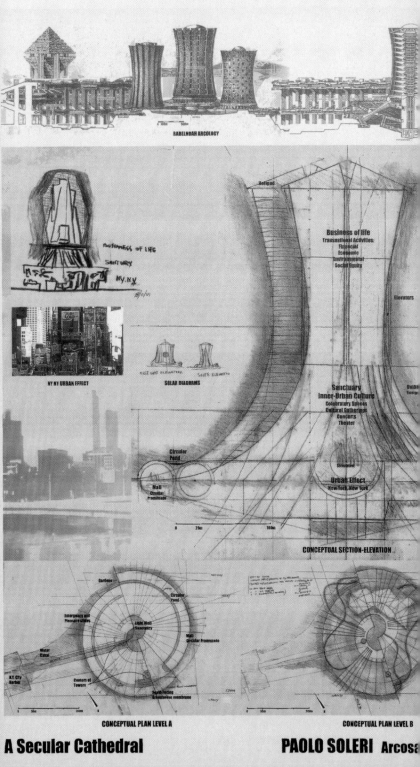

BABELNOAH ARCOLOGY

Retinal

Business of life
Transnational Activities:
Financial
Economic
Environmental
Social Equity

Elevators

BUSINESS OF LIFE
SANCTUARY
NY. N.Y.

NY NY URBAN EFFECT

SOLAR DIAGRAMS

Sanctuary
Inner-Urban Culture
Celebratory Spaces
Cultural Gatherings
Concerts
Theater

Circular
Pond

Mall
Circular
Promenade

Urban Effect
New York, New York

0   25m   100m

CONCEPTUAL SECTION-ELEVATION

Gardens

Circular
Pond

Emergency and
Pleasure slides

Light Well
Sanctuary

Mall
Circular Promenade

Water
Canal

N.Y. City
Harbor

Centers of
Towers

South Facing
Greenhouse membrane

CONCEPTUAL PLAN LEVEL A

CONCEPTUAL PLAN LEVEL B

A Secular Cathedral

PAOLO SOLERI Arcosa

Born in Italy, Paolo Soleri came to the United States in 1947 to work with Frank Lloyd Wright. In 1956 he settled in Scottsdale, Arizona, and began a lifelong commitment to experimentation in urban planning. In 1970 he began work on Arcosanti, a prototype town for five thousand people. Located at Cordes Junction in central Arizona, the project is based on Soleri's concept of "Arcology," which envisions an architecture coherent with ecology.

Paolo Soleri

The Secular Cathedral

My proposal is for a transnational structure aiming at a distant, more equitable consumerism, and a habitat for remembering, living, working, learning, and "divertimento." Part of the divertimento is the battery of slides evacuating the cathedral in twenty minutes or so (twenty thousand people?). The mantle generated by the forty or so slides defines an umbrella-parasol of about four hundred meters diameter covering a multistory urban life that the citizens of New York would think about and the designer-builder would try to satisfy (the analogy with the Piero della Francesca generous mantle of mother sheltering the flock of her children). The circular pond is the speed breaker for the people evacuating the cathedral from most of its stories. The evacuation is pure gravity-effect descent, with no mechanical equipment, no energy use, in fact no need of leg use. It is a very large combination of children's playground and swimming pool slide, of roller-coaster rides and of emergency slides in passenger airplanes. From floor 30 one would be able to reach a restaurant or a shop on Barclay Street, West Street, Liberty Street, etc., in less than one minute. This is part of the appeal offered by the multilevel grounds of the cathedral to visitors and employees. Magnetic levitation propulsion is suggested for the power-driven ascent conveyances. Besides escalators and elevators, gondolas could be propelled on wider slides.

The first four to five floors are of the "New York, New York" format; the typical busybody goings-about of Manhattan's people. Those floors ring the area and also serve as entrance to the inner urban-celebratory spaces where business, cultural gatherings, concerts, and theater let the visitors commingle, enjoy, and learn. This is a multistory inner space under the cover of the slides and umbrella-parasol. Simulacra made of some of the structural segments of the towers might be afloat where the centers of the two towers used to be. The remaining floors, forty to fifty, are for the transitional activities in financial, economic, environmental, and social equity fields of endeavor.

Michael Sorkin is principal of the Michael Sorkin Studio in New York City, a design practice devoted to both practical and theoretical projects. The studio's work has been exhibited in many museums and public institutions in both the United States and abroad. Recent design projects include a master plan for a transit hub in the Bronx and a project for a zero-emissions incinerator and ecological village in Sendai, Japan.

Michael Sorkin Studio

Disaggregation

Given the probable level of investment available for reconstructing lower Manhattan, the current soft office market, and the likely long-term needs of the city as a whole, it seems logical to question the hasty reconstruction of very large amounts of office space on or near Ground Zero. Instead, this plan suggests that a far more comprehensive plan be developed to vitalize other centers throughout the city which stand to benefit dramatically from fresh infusions of capital and space. Such local centers would provide highly sustainable, walkable environments and reinforce neighborhoods—like Jamaica, Flushing, or the Bronx Hub—that already have strong character, community, and connections. Of course, any such development should be strongly mixed, bringing new housing, commercial, and cultural development along with office space.

Ground Zero

Ground Zero is a sacred place, as charged with memories and aura as Gettysburg, Babi Yar, or New York City's African Burial Ground. This proposal suggests a modest beginning, an earthen berm surrounding the site, providing protection from demolition and reconstruction, as well as a platform for public viewing. Eventually, this berm might become permanent, harboring a shallow green crater, an Elysian Field in perpetual memory of the fallen, and a site for more particular memorials. More important, though, is a long reflection about Ground Zero's future. The berm

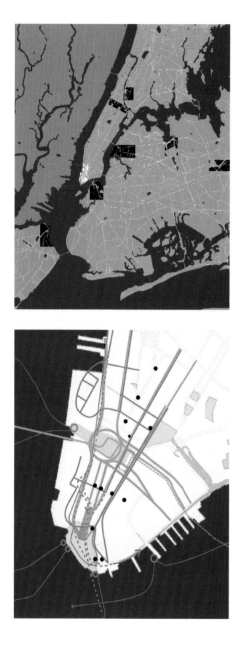

and field might simply serve as a placeholder for what can only be decided after long deliberation and the most thorough contest of ideas.

West Street

West Street is an intimidating barrier dividing Battery Park City from the rest of the island, forcing pedestrians onto bridges and denying pleasant uses at its edges. Rebuilding West Street underground from Harrison Street south to the Battery Tunnel would take traffic off local streets, permitting a green seam to stitch the fabric of lower Manhattan back together, permanently eliminating through traffic and providing new opportunities for recreation and sociability.

Intermodal Transit Hub

The proposal replaces a portion of the yacht harbor at the World Financial Center with a covered ferry terminal linked to a rebuilt winter garden. This, in turn, would be connected to the PATH and subways to create a continuous Intermodal Transit Hub and shopping center beneath the site, perhaps eventually including a Long Island Rail Road connection. An expanded version of this scheme imagines alteration of the West Side piers to permit circulation of water taxis and buses along the bulkhead line and allow for the development of additional waterfront recreational space.

Greenfill

Lower Manhattan is an ideal place for walkers and this plan proposes a substantial reclamation of street space for pedestrian and "slo-mo" circulation. For this, Ground Zero might become a point of dissemination for this new network, which itself might be a model for the recovery from the car of the public realm throughout New York. This greenfill might begin with appropriations along Broadway, Church Street, Greenwich Street, Chambers Street, Fulton Street, John Street, and Vesey Street.

Downtown Campus

There is a concentration of academic institutions, including Borough of Manhattan Community College, St. John's

University, Stuyvesant High School, and several intermediate and elementary schools that form the core of a potential downtown campus. The suppression of West Street offers the opportunity to create a series of open spaces, linking this collection of schools into a continuous place and providing the community and schools with additional green and athletic space. In the midst of this complex would lie the "Quint" a five-sided central space for the campus.

Building Opportunities

Although this scheme is predicated on disaggregation—the construction of replacement office space on sites scattered around the city—there are nonetheless many building opportunities throughout lower Manhattan. In addition to sites on terra firma, the east side of the island also provides many opportunities for pier-based construction and the revival of an active commercial waterfront. This plan suggests office space, housing, and marine activities—either as low-rise structures or as skinny towers—on new and reconstructed piers along the southern rim of the island.

The Lawn

By burying the Battery Tunnel approach and demolishing the large municipal parking structure to its west, an opportunity is created for a dramatic new civic space, a lawn extending from Rector Street to Battery Park and offering sites for new development along its edges, like a miniature Central Park. The tunnel approach would be linked directly to an underground West Street, calming a large quadrant of the island.

Hydrologic Fill

The biological dead zone created by the squared-off configuration of the north end of the Battery Park City landfill is redressed by additional fill which smoothes, aerates, and cleanses the flow of the Hudson. The landfill would also provide substantial additional recreational space in an area of New York poorly provisioned with it.

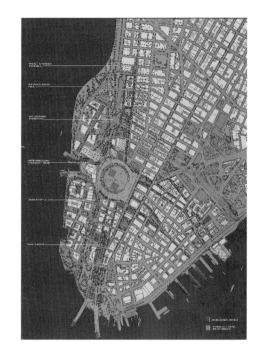

A New World Trade Center
Design Proposal

Two new towers ascend thinner
and taller from the slipped
footprint of the original
World Trade Center towers.
Steel and mirror glass, they
reflect orange at dawn and
at sunset.

Light baths the skin of the
towers and projects up to the
money god.

The towers rise from a memory
of the ruins.

Where the towers touch the
earth, two memorials descend
from the footprints of the
World Trade Center.

One third of one building lobby
is a rectangular pool of water.
One third of the other is a
floor of mirror.

The memorials descend as deep
as the original World Trade
Center towers were high.
One is a shaft of water. The
other a kaleidoscope of mirror.
Both are lit from 110 stories
below.

Barbara Stauffacher Solomon
and
Nellie King Solomon

Barbara Stauffacher Solomon, artist, designer, and author, studied art at the San Francisco Art Institute and design at the Kunstgewerbeschule in Basel, and holds a B.A. in history and an M. Arch. from the University of California at Berkeley. A 1983 fellow at the American Academy in Rome and winner of the 1990 NEA Distinguished Designer Fellowship. Artist Nellie King Solomon studied architecture at Cooper Union in New York and holds a B.A. from the University of California at Santa Cruz and an M.F.A. from CCAC in San Francisco. She worked in architectural restoration in Venice and as an architect for Ricardo Bofill in Barcelona. Recently, King Solomon has had solo shows of her paintings at the Branstein/Quay Gallery in San Francisco, Julie Baker/Fine Arts in Grass Valley, California, and Dennis Ochi Gallery in Sun Valley, Utah.

Barbara Stauffacher Solomon & Nellie King Solomon

Ascending Towers, Descending Memorials

The new towers ascend thinner and taller from the slipped footprint of the original World Trade Center towers. Steel and mirror glass, they reflect orange at dawn and at sunset.

Light bathes the skin of the towers and projects up to the money god.

The towers rise from a memory of the ruins. Where the towers touch the earth, two memorials descend from the footprints of the World Trade Center.

One third of one building lobby is a rectangular pool of water. One third of the other is a floor of mirror.

The memorials descend as deep as the original World Trade Center towers were high. One is a shaft of water. The other is a kaleidoscope of mirror. Both are lit from 110 stories below.

A Tribute in Light

These images represent a joint initiative by John Bennett, Gustavo Bonevardi, Julian LaVerdiere, Paul Marantz, Paul Myoda and Richard Nash-Gould, with organizing support from the Municipal Art Society, and Creative Time.

Together this team developed a collaborative proposal for a temporary art installation, conceived in the aftermath of the September 11 tragedies. Designed as a gift for New York City and its public, it consisted of twin white beacons of light that rose from lower Manhattan as a symbol of strength, hope, and resiliency; a reclamation of New York City's skyline and identity; a tribute to rescue workers; and a mnemonic for all those who lost their lives. Located adjacent to the World Trade Center site in an empty lot, this public installation neither interfered with nor detracted from recovery efforts, debris removal, and reconstruction. Rather, the project was an immediate and temporary artistic gesture proposed to foster hope, unity, healing, and comprehension of the mass devastation suffered on September 11 by New York City and the world at large.

On the evening of March 11, 2002, the proposal described above became a reality as two great beams of light rose from lower Manhattan. As realized, Tribute in Light was the result of an extensive dialogue with victims' families, neighborhood residents, and public officials, as well as a technical collaboration between dozens of individuals and organizations. For the month that the lights illuminated the New York sky, they were experienced by millions throughout the metropolitan region and beyond. The organizers are deeply grateful to all those whose work and donations made this unique project possible.

John Bennett was born and raised in Clarksburg, West Virginia. He received his B.A. from Oberlin College in 1990 and his M. Arch. from Columbia University in 1993. He has taught at New York's School of Visual Arts and the Parsons Graduate School of Architecture.

Gustavo Bonevardi was born and raised in New York City. He received his A.B. from Sarah Lawrence College in 1983 and his M. Arch. from Princeton University in 1986. He has taught at the Universidad Nacional de Buenos Aires and Universidad Nacional de Cordoba in Argentina as well as the Parsons Graduate School of Architecture.

Julian LaVerdiere was born in 1971 and raised in New York City. He received his B.F.A. in 1993 from the Cooper Union and his M.F.A. from the Yale Graduate School of Sculpture in 1995. LaVerdiere presently lives and works in New York City and is represented by the Lehmann Maupin Gallery, New York; No Limits Gallery, Milan; and the EverGreen Gallery, Geneva. LaVerdiere has exhibited his work at P.S. 1, the Museum of Modern Art, and the New Museum in New York; Miami's Museum of Contemporary Art; the Tang Museum in Saratoga, New York; Museé de L'Elysée in Lausanne, Switzerland; and Artium Vitoria-gasteiz in Spain.

Paul Myoda was born in Wilmington, Delaware. For his B.F.A., Myoda attended the Rhode Island School of Design, after which the artist received his M.F.A. from Yale University's Graduate School of Art in 1994. He is based in Manhattan and represented there by Friedrich Petzel Gallery. Myoda has exhibited artworks nationally and internationally, and has written for various art and cultural publications.

Laverdiere & Myoda collaboratively received a Warhol Foundation Grant and a research laboratory grant at the Museum of Natural History in 2000, and a Lower Manhattan Cultural Council studio grant in World Trade Center 1 in the spring of 2001, all on behalf of their Bioluminescent Beacon Project.

Richard Nash-Gould has been the sole proprietor of his own architectural practice in New York City since 1980. Where there is darkness, let there be light.

Creative Time is a nonprofit arts organization in New York City, which, for nearly thirty years, has presented adventurous public art projects of all disciplines. From the Brooklyn Bridge Anchorage, Grand Central Terminal, and Times Square to milk cartons, billboards, and skywriting over New York City, Creative Time has a long and distinguished history of commissioning and presenting art that enhances the public realm.

The Municipal Art Society is a private, nonprofit membership organization whose mission is to promote a more livable city. Grand Central Terminal, Radio City Music Hall, Times Square, historic Greenwich Village, count-less monuments and murals in public places, and the landmarks law itself all exist and or have been protected because of the Municipal Art Society.

Marion Weiss and Michael Manfredi established Weiss/Manfredi Architects, based in New York and known for its dynamic integration of architecture, art, infrastructure, and landscape design. It was named one of the six "critical emerging practices" in North America by the Architectural League of New York. Among Weiss and Manfredi's most recently built projects are competition-winning designs for the Olympia Fields Park and Community Center and Women's Memorial and Education Center at Arlington National Cemetery. They are currently designing the Seattle Art Museum Sculpture Park and the Greentree Foundation's Center for Peace in New York.

Weiss/Manfredi Architects

Reflect/Remember

The magnitude of this loss defies quick solutions. We question what kind of connection to the physical world will preserve the memory of this loss. Things that are immaterial are given measure in many different ways. In our drawing, the reflection of the World Trade Center is a poem—a tribute. This is not a strategy or a proposal, but homage to something lost that can be captured only through the most ephemeral means. The horizon now is seen without the towers, but perhaps a reflection might hold them forever.

Design is our mission, our passion, our art, but to realize the full potential of constructing this site, we feel the imperative to ask questions first. How can we consider the vacancy on the horizon before we impose a new vision? Is there a form of construction that will not eradicate the events of September 11? How can the immensity of this event remain evident without adopting the imperative of immense development?

Should there be a period of mourning before we market solutions? Where does memory end, where does construction begin?

The work of Tod Williams Billie Tsien and Associates bridges different worlds—joining theory and practice, architecture and the fine arts. Their built work, bordering on minimalism, pays careful attention to context, to detail, and to the subtleties of a subdued but rich materiality. Major buildings include the Neurosciences Institute in La Jolla, California, the Phoenix Art Museum, the Cranbrook Natatorium in Bloomfield Hills, Michigan, and the Mattin Art Center, a fifty-five-thousand-square-foot student arts building recently opened at Johns Hopkins University. A new thirty-five thousand-square-foot building for the Museum of American Folk Art in New York City was completed in December 2001.

Tod Williams Billie Tsien

Buildings in the Form of Trees

The two drawings are thoughts about possibilities. The first is in the image of a grouping of trees. The thought is that the buildings could be branched and joined to each other at the upper levels. Like trees, the structure/space below ground goes deep and spreads wide. The second suggests a grouping of several slender towers ringing the edge of the World Trade Center site. Perhaps this too is something of an abstraction of trees, in this case involving a clearing. Two-thirds up, a wide band of public space wraps and connects all the buildings. This also is the place of a public plaza. The central core is open, leaving the site in the center open to the sky and empty.

Mehrdad Yazdani is design principal of CannonDesign and director of the firm's YazdaniStudio. In 1994, the *Los Angeles Times Magazine* featured him as one of the ten leading architectural talents in southern California, and in 2000, he was named one of Los Angeles's twenty-five most highly regarded designers by the *Los Angeles Business Journal*. Recent award-winning work has included the Lloyd D. George U.S. Courthouse in Las Vegas, Nevada, and the El Sereno Recreation Center and Santa Monica/Vermont Metro Station in Los Angeles.

Mehrdad Yazdani

A Center for the Humanities

An idea for the reconstruction of the site of the World Trade Center is to create architecture that stitches the site back into the city's fabric while maintaining the footprint of the Twin Towers as memorial sites for victims of the September 11 incident.

In contrast to the previous World Trade Center complex, which was comprised of autonomous buildings surrounding an open space, this idea proposes to build at the center of the site, at the confluence of all of the adjacent streets, thus reconnecting the site to its urban context. It will become a center for the humanities, and will house a museum, libraries, and conference venues. It will form a space for discourse on the causes and effects of global terrorism and on how to unite humankind.

The multistory, mixed-use urban block fills the majority of the site, leaving the imprints of the Twin Towers as memorial sites. The block is sculpted to challenge the rhythm of Manhattan's urban walls, and to remind us of the uniqueness of this site within the city. Rising above these blocks are clusters of office and residential towers, which differ from the original identical Twin Towers and celebrate diversity in their multiplicity of form and orientation. This variety of expression recognizes our differences while maintaining our unity.

The two memorial sites become "living links" that connect across to the water through twin gardens, proportioned after the length of the Twin Towers and reminiscent of their shadows. This recalls the destruction of the towers yet allows nature and life to take form in their absence.

Architect Information and Project Credits

Max Protetch Gallery
511 West 22nd Street
New York, NY 10011
212-633-6999
info@maxprotetch.com
www.maxprotetch.com

Balthazar Korab
Korab Photo
4104 42nd Avenue South
Minneapolis, MN 55406
612-729-2907

1100 Architect
David Piscuskas and Juergen
  Reihm
435 Hudson Street
New York, NY 10014
212-645-1011
contact@1100architect.com
www.1100architect.com

Raimund Abraham
44 Bond Street
New York, NY 10012
212-254-3537
fax 212-254-3696

Acconci Studio
Vito Acconci, Dario Nunez,
  Peter Dorsey, Stephen Roe,
  Sergio Prego, Gia Wolff
55 Washington Street
Brooklyn, NY 11201
718-852-6591
studio@acconci.com
www.acconci.com

Morris Adjmi
45 East 20th Street
New York, NY 10003
212-982-4700 x234
ma@ma.com
www.ma.com

Marwan Al-Sayed
4411 North 40th Street, #56
Phoenix, AZ 85018
602-912-9350
info@masastudio.com
www.masastudio.com

Allied Works Architecture
Brad Cloepfil
2768 NW Thurman Street
Portland, OR 97210
503-227-1737
info@alliedworks.com
www.alliedworks.com

Will Alsop
41 Parkgate Road
London SW11 4NP
England
44-207-978-7878
info@alsoparchitects.com
www.alsoparchitects.com

Archi-Tectonics
Principal in Charge: Winka
  Dubbeldam
Project Team: Seiichi Saito,
  Sangkyun Im, Leo Yung
Investment Consulting:
  Jonathan Carroll
Sound Design: Emanuel
  Ruffler
Sponsor (exhibition units):
  United Aluminum Door,
  New York
111 Mercer Street
New York, NY 10012
212-226-0303
info@archi-tectonics.com
www.archi-tectonics.com

Asymptote
Hani Rashid
561 Broadway
Suite 5A
New York, NY 10012
212-343-7333
info@asymptote.net
www.asymptote.net

Shigeru Ban
5-2-4 Matsubara Ban
  Building
1st Floor
Setagaya, Tokyo 156
Japan
81-3-3324-6760
SBA@tokyo.email.ne.jp

Carlos Brillembourg
73 Spring Street
New York, NY 10021
212-431-4597
brillembourg@mindspring.com
www.carlosbrillembourg.com

Mel Chin
Conceptual Contributors:
  John Abernathy, Barron
  Brown, Nick Dryden, Mark
  L. Gardner, Stephen
  McRedmond, Tamalyn
  Miller, Julie Torres-
  Moskovitz, Helen K.
  Nagge
P.O. Box 566
Burnsville, NC 28714
melchin@aol.com

Preston Scott Cohen
  with K+D Lab
Harvard Design School
48 Quincy Street
Cambridge, MA 02138
617-817-0728
scohen@gsd.harvard.edu
www.gsd.harvard.edu

Coop Himmelb(l)au
Zelinkgasse 2/4
A-1010 Vienna
Austria
43-1-532-55-35
office@coop-himmelblau.at
www.coop-himmelblau.at

Della Valle + Bernheimer
  Design
70 Washington Street
Suite 808
Brooklyn, NY 11201
718-222-8155
abernheimer@d-bd.com
www.d-bd.com

Field Operations
Stan Allen and James Corner
270 Water Street
New York, NY 10039
212-233-0357
www.fieldoperations.net

Foreign Office Architects
58 Belgrade Road
London SW1V 2BP
England
44-207-976-5988
mail@f-o-a.net
www.f-o-a.net

Fox & Fowle
Design Principal: Daniel
  Kaplan, AIA
Project Team: David Ennis II,
  David Enriquez, Xander
  Redfern
22 West 19th Street
11th Floor
New York, NY 10011
212-627-1700
ksibilia@foxfowle.com
www.foxfowle.com

Joseph Giovannini & Rodrigo
  Monsalve
140 East 40th Street, #11E
New York, NY 10016
212-297-0980
fax 212-297-1850

Gluckman Mayner Architects
  Richard Gluckman and
  Srdjan Jovanovic Weiss
250 Hudson Street
New York, NY 10013
212-929-0100
info@gluckmanmayner.com
www.gluckmanmayner.com

Alexander Gorlin Architects
  Alexander Gorlin and
  Brendan Cotter
137 Varick Street
5th Floor
New York, NY 10013
212-229-1199
agorlin@gorlinarchitect.com
www.gorlinarchitect.com

Michael Graves & Associates
341 Nassau Street
Princeton, NJ 08540
609-924-6409
www.michaelgraves.com

Zaha Hadid
10 Bowling Green Lane
Studio 9
London EC1
England
44-207-253-4157
mail@zaha-hadid.com
www.zaha-hadid.com

Hugh Hardy
902 Broadway
19th Floor
New York, NY 10010
212-677-6030
slasoff@hhpa.com
www.hhpa.com

Hariri & Hariri
18 East 12th Street
New York, NY 10003
212-727-0338
info@haririandhariri.com
www.haririandhariri.com

Hodgetts + Fung Design
    Associates
5837 Adams Street
Culver City, CA 90232
323-937-2150
mail@hplusf.com
www.hplusf.com

Steven Holl
    with Makram El-Kadi and
    Ziad Jameleddine
450 West 31st Street
11th Floor
New York, NY 10001
212-629-7262
mail@stevenholl.com
www.stevenholl.com

Hans Hollein
Argentinierstrasse 36
1040 Vienna
Austria
43-1-505-5196
fax 43-1-505-8894

Jakob + MacFarlane
13 rue des Petites Ecu Ries
Paris 75010
France
33-1-4479-0572
jakmak@club-internet.fr

Eytan Kaufman Design and
    Development
Design Associate: Andrea
    Ljahnicky
Computer Imaging: Martin
    Newton
101 5th Avenue
New York, NY 10003
212-691-1607
Eytandesign@hotmail.com

Kennedy & Violich
160 North Washington
    Street, #814
Boston, MA 02114
617-367-3784
fviolich@kvarch.net
www.kvarch.net

Tom Kovac
Design Team: Jonathan
    Podborsek, Roland Snooks
Digital Imaging: Jack Hanane
13/410 Queen Street
Melbourne, VIC 3000
Australia
61-412-110-189
kovactom@hotmail.com

Krueck & Sexton
Design Principal: Ronald
    Kruek
Design Team: Nemish Shah,
    Parus Kiravanich
221 West Erie Street
Chicago, IL 60610
312-787-0056
admin@ksarch.com
www.ksarch.com

Daniel Libeskind
Kurfurstendamm 96
Berlin D-10709
Germany
49-30-327-782-61
info@daniel-libeskind.com
www.daniel-libeskind.com

LOT-EK
55 Little West 12th Street
New York, NY 10014
212-255-9326
info@lot-ek.com
www.lot-ek.com

Greg Lynn FORM
1402 Oakwood Avenue
Venice, CA 90291
310-821-2629
node@GLFORM.com
www.glform.com

Iñigo Manglano-Ovalle
Max Protetch Gallery
511 West 22nd Street
New York, NY 10011
212-633-6999
info@maxprotetch.com
www.maxprotetch.com

Nathan McRae
Keenen/Riley
526 West 26th Street, #9A
New York, NY 10001
212-645-9210
nm@krnyc.com

Samuel Mockbee
Max Protetch Gallery
511 West 22nd Street
New York, NY 10011
212-633-6999
info@maxprotetch.com
www.maxprotetch.com

Morphosis
2041 Colorado Avenue
Santa Monica, CA 90404
310-453-2247
studio@morphosis.net
www.morphosis.net

Eric Owen Moss
8557 Higuera Street
Culver City, CA 90232
310-839-1199
mail@ericowenmoss.com
www.ericowenmoss.com

Ben Nicholson
4025 North Hermitage
Chicago, IL 60613
773-883-1905
comma@suba.com

NOX
Lars Spuybroek with Chris
    Seung-woo Yoo and Kris
    Mun
Matnesseriaan 443
3023 GJ Rotterdam
Netherlands
31-10-477-2853
nox@luna.nl

OCEAN north
Project Coordinators: Michael
    Hensel, Birger Sevaldson
Project Contributors: Lip-
    Khoon Chiong, Morten
    Gregersen, Achim Menges,
    Jeff Turko
Video Rendering: Kim
    Baumann Larsen
Modeling: Are Neilsen
Meritullinkau 11
00170 Helsinki
Finland
358-9-278-3602
info@ocean-north.org
www.ocean-net.org

Office dA
Monica Ponce de Leon,
    Nader Tehrani, Hansy Luz
    Better, Hamad Al Sultan,
    Christine Mueller,
    Christopher Orsega,
    Timothy Clark, Albert
    Garcia, Achille Rossini, Tali
    Buchler, Kristen
    Giannattasio, Jeffrey
    Asanza
575 Concord Street, #6
Boston, MA 02118
617-267-7369
da@officeda.com
www.officeda.com

Oosterhuis.nl
Essenburgsingel 94c
3022 EG Rotterdam
Netherlands
31-10-244-7039
oosterhuis@oosterhuis.nl
www.oosterhuis.nl

Frei Otto
Passenwaldring 14
7000 Stuttgart 80
Germany
49-71-524-1084
fax 49-7-1524-3908

Marjetica Potrč
Max Protetch Gallery
511 West 22nd Street
New York, NY 10011
212-633-6999
info@maxprotetch.com
www.maxprotetch.com

RoTo Architects
600 Moulton Avenue, #405
Los Angeles, CA 90031
323-226-1112
roto@rotoark.com
www.rotoark.com

SITE
James Wines, Denise McLee,
    Stomu Miyasaki, Patrick
    Head, Sara Stracey
25 Maiden Lane
2nd Floor
New York, NY 10038
212-285-0120
info@siteenvirodesign.com
www.siteenvirodesign.com

Paolo Soleri
Arcosanti HC 74, Box 4136
Mayer, AZ 86333
928-632-6201
arcodesign@arcosanti.org
www.arcosanti.org

Michael Sorkin Studio
Project Team: Michael Sorkin,
    Jair Laiter, Gustavo
    Gonzales, Catherine
    Martin
145 Hudson Street, 14th Floor
New York, NY 10013
212-241-9120
sorkin@thing.net
www.thing.net/~sorkin/

Barbara Stauffacher Solomon
30 Bellair Place
San Francisco, CA 94133
415-421-4619

Nellie King Solomon
4 Winfield Street
San Francisco, CA 94110
415-821-1608
nellieking@earthlink.net

Towers of Light/Tribute in Light
John Bennett
Gustavo Bonevardi
Proun Studio
799 Greenwich Street
New York, NY 10014
info@proun.com
www.proun.com

Richard Nash-Gould
141 Wooster Street
New York, NY 10012
212-473-1290
rng@rngarchitects.com
www.rngarchitects.com

Julian LaVerdiere
Paul Myoda
Big Room
560 West 29th Street
New York, NY 10001
julian@bigroom.net
Myoda67@aol.com

Weiss/Manfredi Architects
130 West 29th Street
12th Floor
New York, NY 10001
212-431-8255
weiss-
manfredi@worldnet.att.net

Tod Williams Billie Tsien
222 Central Park South
New York, NY 10019
212-582-2385
fax 212-245-1984
www.twbta.com

Mehrdad Yazdani
Yazdani Studio
1901 Avenue of the Stars,
    #13175
Los Angeles, CA 90067
310-229-2700 x2776
www.yazdanistudio.com

Acknowledgments

I would like to thank Josie Browne, director of the gallery, who essentially ran the gallery during the months required to prepare for the exhibition; Stuart Krimko, assistant director of the gallery, who worked tirelessly to coordinate the show and realize this book; and the staff members at the gallery who have invested their time and energy in this endeavor: Jennifer Riffle, archivist; James Barber, preparator; and Chris Davison, registrar.

I would also like to thank Sara Amelar and Robert Ivy of *Architectural Record,* Reed Kroloff formerly of *Architecture* magazine, and Aaron Betsky of the Netherlands Architecture Institute for their suggestions of architects to include in the exhibition, as well as Thomas Mellins, who provided valuable support during the compilation of this book.

Of course I am also most grateful to the architects and artists who agreed to participate, and whose contributions were the essence of the show.

The exhibition that was the basis for this book is dedicated to Samuel Mockbee (1944–2001). Through his work, Sam demonstrated a compassion that will continue to inspire the practice of architecture.